Many people are unaware...

that services of a qualified travel agent do not increase your cost to travel. Quite the contrary.

Travel agents are compensated by the travel providers and make their livings by helping people make the right connections in a more efficient way.

At no cost to you, travel agents help find travel arrangements that meet your specific needs.

Through the efforts of travel agents, travel companies are able to spend less on publicizing their products. Travelers are helped to find the best travel arrangements. The overall result is savings for everyone involved. Travel agents *add value* to the process.

For you, the traveler with a disability, the choice of a good, qualified travel agent who understands your needs is especially critical.

A good travel agent will save you money, but, more importantly, a good travel agent will help make your travel experience more functional and enjoyable.

HOW TO TRAVEL

A GUIDEBOOK
FOR
PERSONS WITH A DISABILITY

By

Fred Rosen

Travel Consultant
for Persons with a Disability

Science & Humanities Press
PO Box 7151
Chesterfield, MO 63006-7151

Graphics Credits:

MasterClips

1895 Francisco Blvd. East, San Rafael, CA 94901

Cover, pages 1, 17, 69

Corel Gallery

1600 Carling Avenue, Ottawa, Ontario Canada K12 8R7

Cover, pages 29, 39, 49, 57, 73, 81

ISBN 1-888725-05-2

Library of Congress

Catalog Card Number: 97-066325

First Printing, March, 1997

Science &
Humanities Press

PO Box 7151
Chesterfield, MO 63006-7151
(636) 394-4950

FOREWORD

There are about 43 million persons in the USA with some form of disability. Many of these people are concerned that they may not be able to enjoy the same activities, such as travel, that people without a disability do. This book is written as a guidebook to your rights and will present information on how to travel to accommodate various disabilities.

Prior to 1986, little or no attention was paid to a person with a disability who wanted to travel. Since 1986, two acts have been passed by the Congress of the United States mandating that travel should be made equally available to all persons, disabled or not.

The first act, the **Air Carriers Access Act (ACAA)**, passed in 1986, defined what air carriers and airports must do to make aircraft and airports accessible to persons with disabilities.

The second act, the **Americans With Disabilities Act (ADA) of 1990**, defined, among its many regulations, what public transportation and accommodations must offer to make their facilities accessible to persons with disabilities. The Act also states that facilities must be made accessible if it is not too difficult or expensive. The ADA does not mandate that the facilities be made usable.

These two acts have made it easier for persons with disabilities to travel, but have not solved all the problems. We hope that in the near future all forms of travel and accommodations will become available and fully accessible for all people regardless of their disability.

Acknowledgment

This guidebook is dedicated to the millions of persons in the USA with disabilities who wish to travel. Not disabled persons, but persons with a disability. To say that you are someone who is disabled implies that you are incapable of performing or acting on your own. Having a disability only signifies that you're limited in what you can or cannot do.

I Wish To Thank:

My wife, Gertrude, for her input and support.

The staff at Hausler Travel Associates, St. Louis, Missouri, for their encouragement

Virginia Baber

Nora Faifer

Michel Schmidt

Dennise Lafferre

The United States Congress for:

- The Air Carriers Access Act of 1986
- The Americans With Disabilities Act of 1990

The US Department of Transportation publication:

"New Horizons For The Disabled Traveler" 1991

The Delta Steamboat Company

National Railroad Passenger Corporation AMTRAK

Greyhound Lines, Inc.

Cruise Lines International Association (CLIA)

American Lung Association

HOW TO TRAVEL

A GUIDEBOOK

FOR

PERSONS WITH A DISABILITY

CONTENTS

I PREFACE

The Boy Scouts of America have a motto, "BE PREPARED". This also applies to you, the traveler with a disability. BE PREPARED. Regardless of the mode of transportation or destination, there are certain things for you to consider before traveling:

- Your medical needs.
- The use of credit cards.
- Whether you need a traveling companion.
- Whether you need a wheelchair.
- How to handle insulin if you are diabetic.
- What to do if you have the need for oxygen.
- Assuring availability of ethnic or dietary foods.
- Transportation of a needed assistive device.
- Assuring assistance if you are hearing impaired.
- Assuring assistance if you are visually impaired.
- Accommodations for a service animal.
- Advisability of purchasing extra medical insurance.
- Importance of cancellation insurance.

Planning to travel is a two-way street. It involves a partnership between the traveler with a disability and the travel industry. Both you and your travel agent should work together in securing the accessibility and accommodations you need. But even with all the proper preparations, sometimes things can go wrong. This guidebook is written to cover these consideration as well as other aspects of travel such as destinations and dining out.

Fred Rosen, Travel Consultant For Persons With A Disability

CHAPTER II

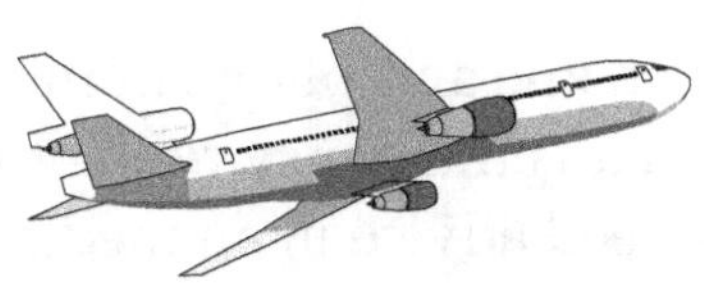

AIR TRAVEL (USA)

In 1986, the United States Congress passed the *Air Carriers Access Act* which mandates that air travel shall be accessible for persons with disabilities. This Act applies only to US air carriers. A person with a disability should know how to prepare for travel by air.

Before Traveling

Check with your physician to see if your condition will permit you to travel.

If your physician gives his or her consent that you can travel, then get a written statement concerning your medical condition, allergies to medication and your current treatment.

Purchase low-cost accident, sickness, baggage, and trip cancellation insurance to protect your investment. The cost of this insurance will more than offset the price if you have to cancel your tour in the event of emergency. Your travel agent should have the necessary forms to purchase insurance.

Things You Will Need

- ☐ A copy of your prescriptions in case you should need an emergency refill;
- ☐ Two sets of medication. Carry one set with you and the other set in your luggage;
- ☐ Enough medication to last a few days longer than your planned trip;
- ☐ Your physician's name and phone number in case you should need an emergency refill of your prescription or need advice in an medical emergency;
- ☐ An extra pair of prescription eyeglasses;
- ☐ Extra batteries if you are hearing impaired.

Travel Tips

Decide where you want to go and when you want to go. Try to make your travel plans as far in advance as possible.

Contact a travel agent to make your arrangements. Inform the travel agent the nature of your disability and of your needs.

Try to book non-stop flights to avoid changing planes. If you are unable to book a non-stop flight, consider a direct flight which makes stops but does not require a change of planes.

If you must change planes, be sure there is enough time between connections.

> NOTE: If you are making your own booking with an airline, get the name and the location of the reservationist you are talking to in case of a problem.

Request bulkhead seating for more leg-room and comfort if you have a mobility problem. You may be denied bulkhead seating if your disability would prevent you from evacuating the aircraft in an emergency.

Use an airline that has advanced reserved seating.

Arrive at the airport well before your departure to allow time to check in. If you are a wheelchair passenger or a passenger using oxygen, you must get to the airport at least one and half hour before departure.

If you have a mobility problem and are unable to walk long distances, arrange for curbside wheelchair service so that you can be transported to your departure gate.

Use the restrooms at the air terminal prior to your departure for more comfort and convenience during your flight.

Avoid alcoholic drinks and heavy meals during the flight.

Remove your shoes, if possible, during the flight as feet have a tendency to swell at higher altitudes.

Consider traveling with a companion to assist you in your needs.

Carry a current major credit card.

Denial Of Transportation

You cannot be denied transportation because of your disability whether it is physical, a lack of mobility, appearance, or involuntary behavior except for the following reasons:

- Your disability poses a threat or danger to the health and safety of other passengers.
- You have a communicable or infectious disease.

- Your seating violates the FAA Exit Row Seating rule. These seats are limited to passengers who can effectively assist in an evacuation if the need arises.
- The aircraft has fewer than 30 seats and there are no boarding devices. Carrier personnel are not required to hand carry a passenger with a disability aboard the aircraft.

If You Are Denied Transportation

If you are denied transportation because of your disability, you can request the services of a Complaints Resolution Officer (CRO) at the airport to mediate the problem.

If you are still denied transportation, the air carrier must furnish you a statement explaining the reason for denial within 10 days of the incident.

If all efforts fail, you may appeal to:

Department of Transportation
Office of Consumer Affairs
400 Seventh St., SW
Washington, DC. 20590

When You Are Required To Give Advance Notice

Air carriers may require you to give 48 hours advance notice and check in one hour in advance if:

1. you are transporting an electrically operated wheelchair on an aircraft with fewer than 60 seats.
2. it is necessary to provide hazardous materials packaging for the battery of an electrically operated wheelchair or other assistive devices.
3. you are traveling with a group of 10 or more individuals with disabilities.

4. you need an on-board wheelchair to reach the lavatory.
5. you require medical oxygen on the aircraft during the flight. Prearrangements have to be made with your physician and the airline. You should get a prescription from your physician indicating your need for oxygen and notify your selected air carrier that you will require oxygen during the flight.
6. you are traveling on a stretcher.
7. you are carrying an incubator.
8. you need to connect your respirator to the aircraft's electrical system

NOTE: Air carriers are not required to provide services and equipment for oxygen, stretchers, incubators or respirators, but may do so and charge a fee.

When A Medical Certificate May Be Required

An air carrier may demand a medical certificate if:

- You are on a stretcher or have a baby in an incubator (where such service is provided).
- You have the need for medical oxygen during the flight.
- Your medical condition is such that the air carrier has doubts of whether or not you can complete the flight safely without extraordinary medical assistance during the flight.
- You have a communicable or infectious disease that could be transmitted during the flight.

When An Attendant May Be Required

If you are traveling alone and your condition warrants an attendant, the air carrier may require that you be accompanied by an attendant even if you object, but they cannot charge for the transportation of the attendant. The attendant may be someone of your choice, a volunteer from the passengers aboard the aircraft, or the carrier may assign an off-duty employee. An attendant may be required if you are traveling on a stretcher or in an incubator, you are unable to comprehend or respond to safety instructions from the carrier personnel because of a mental disability, you have a severe mobility impairment that it would prevent you from acting in your own evacuation from the aircraft, or you have both a severe hearing and visual impairment which would prevent you from receiving and acting on necessary instructions from carrier personnel when evacuating the aircraft during an emergency.

Advance Information For The Hearing Impaired

Any carrier that provides telephone service to the general public for the purpose of making reservations and offering information, must provide the same information via TDD/TTY service if you are hearing impaired.

Flight Information At The Airport

If you are visually or hearing impaired, air carriers must provide you, upon request, the same information about flights, departures, arrivals, and gates provided to other passengers.

Security Screening Before Boarding

All passengers are required to undergo a security screening prior to boarding. If you are unable to pass the security system, you can request that the search be done in private.

Safety Briefing Before Departure

All passengers are required, by FAA rules, to be given a safety briefing before departure. If you are visually or hearing impaired, you can request a private briefing if you choose to pre-board.

Boarding And Deplaning The Aircraft

On large and medium aircraft, air carriers must supply you with a boarding device, such as a level ramp or mobile lounge. If a boarding device is not available, the air carrier must provide you with some other means of boarding. Hand carrying a passenger with a disability aboard the aircraft is not recommended.

On aircraft with 30 or fewer seats, carrier personnel do not have to hand carry you aboard but may voluntarily do so.

You cannot be left unattended in your wheelchair or in a boarding wheelchair for more than 30 minutes.

It is recommended that you pre-board, but it isn't required, if you choose not to do so.

It is the air carrier's responsibility to transport you between gates if necessary to assist you in reaching your connecting flights.

Traveling With An Assistive Device

You can bring your ventilator or respirator into the cabin of the aircraft but it must be powered by gel-cells or non-spillable batteries. The device must fit under a seat or be strapped to an adjoining seat. If an adjoining seat is required, it must be purchased.

You must give the carrier 48-hour notice if you are traveling with a ventilator or respirator.

Other devices can be stored in the overhead compartment. If your device is too large for the cabin, then it will be transported in the cargo compartment of the aircraft. If your device is too large to fit into the cargo compartment of the aircraft, it may be disassembled, but it must be returned to you reassembled.

Traveling With Oxygen

Each carrier has its own requirements for a passenger traveling with oxygen. Have your travel agent check on the requirements with the carrier when making your reservation.

If you have the need of medical oxygen during the flight, you must give a carrier 48 hours or more advance notice. You will be required to have a letter and a prescription, in triplicate, from your physician indicating that you are able to travel, you require oxygen and indicate the liter per minute flow.

A carrier can require that you travel with a companion if you need medical oxygen.

You are not allowed to carry filled oxygen tanks on board the aircraft. Your oxygen containers must be purged, free of pressure and sent through as baggage.

Airlines charge a fee for providing medical oxygen by a coupon system. The number of coupons needed to reach your destination depends on how many times you change planes. For example, if you travel from St. Louis to Detroit and change planes in Chicago, you will need two coupons.

Before Departure:

- Tell your travel agent that you need special services.
- Try to book a flight on a week day and during normal business hours of a supplier to make it easier for some one to meet you at the airport with an oxygen supply.
- Have your physician give you a prescription indicating your need for oxygen and the liter-per-minute flowrate. It is recommended that you travel with a portable, self-sustained oxygen system.
- Inform your oxygen supplier of your travel plans. Your supplier can recommend the best system to travel with, make arrangements to have a representative meet you at the airport with oxygen refills and have oxygen equipment at your destination. Airlines do not provide oxygen for ground use. It is your responsibility to make arrangements to have your oxygen tank refilled if you have to change planes or have a lay-over.
- You should have a list of suppliers and their locations, the refill charges, and the form of payment accepted if you will need refills.

The Wheelchair Traveler

Gate Tag

If you need a wheelchair, mechanical or electrical, it is recommended that you check in at your departure gate. Ask for a gate tag which is fluorescent in color. Your wheelchair will be tagged, denoting your destination and alerting the airline not to send your wheelchair through baggage. It will be the last item loaded into the cargo department and the first item unloaded and will be delivered to you when you deplane.

> ***Consider Traveling With A Lightweight, Mechanical, Folding Wheelchair***
>
> Bring extra nuts, bolts and special tools in case you have to dismantle or repair your wheelchair.
>
> Local bicycle shops are a good source for wheelchair spare parts and repairs.

Traveling With A Portable Wheelchair

One folding wheelchair can be stowed in a cabin closet, or in other approved priority storage areas if the aircraft has such areas and storage can be accomplished in accordance with FAA safety regulations. Your wheelchair can be stowed in the cabin closet of the aircraft providing that you pre-board and that it does not protrude into the aisle. Your wheelchair will have priority only over other passengers items boarding with you at the same airport, but not over items from previous stops.

Traveling With A Power Wheelchair

If you are traveling with an power wheelchair, carriers may require that your wheelchair be stowed in the cargo compartment of the aircraft. It is recommended that you use gel-cell or dry-cell batteries which do not have to be removed in stowage. Wet-cell batteries must be removed and properly packaged if your wheelchair cannot be loaded, stored, secured and unloaded in an upright position in the cargo compartment of the aircraft according to the Department of Transportation rules.

Your wheelchair will take priority over other baggage and cargo in the cargo compartment and must be the first item unloaded.

You are not required to sign a waiver of liability for loss or damage to your wheelchair.

Using An On-Board Wheelchair

A carrier must provide an on-board wheelchair if:

- the aircraft has more than 60 seats
- the aircraft has an accessible lavatory.
- the aircraft has an inaccessible lavatory and you have given notice that you can use the lavatory but need an on-board wheelchair to reach it.

Traveling With A Service Animal

You must inform an air carrier that you are traveling with a service animal.

You are permitted to have a service animal accompany you aboard the aircraft at no charge. If your service animal is a guide dog, you should carry its certification and have documentation to show the need for a guide dog.

You must control your guide dog at all times either by a harness, muzzle, leash or verbal command.

The guide dog may accompany you to your seat unless it obstructs the aisle or emergency exits. In that case you will be assigned another seat.

If your service animal is a monkey, it must be caged at all times and the cage fit under the seat in front of you.

Air carriers limit the number of service animals aboard the aircraft for any one flight. Have your travel agent check to assure the limit is not exceeded.

Traveling As A Diabetic

Advise your travel agent that you will need refrigeration on board the aircraft for your insulin. Also carry an extra supply of vials of insulin with you in case of breakage.

The Need For Special And Dietary Foods

You must give the air carrier 24 hours or more advance notice if you require special or ethnic foods.

Specific Seating

You are not required to sit in a particular seat except those prohibited by FAA safety rules such as FAA Exit Row Seating rule.

You can be denied specific seating if you lack sufficient mobility, strength, dexterity, vision, speech, hearing or comprehension ability to perform emergency evacuation functions.

Rather than refusing service, a specific seat can be assigned if your involuntary behavior would compromise the safety of the flight.

If the seat you desire cannot accommodate a guide dog or a service animal the carrier is obligated to find you another seat.

In-Cabin Assistance By Carrier Personnel

Carrier personnel will assist you:

- To move to and from your seat as part of the boarding and exiting process.
- To open packages and identify food but are not required to feed you.
- In the use of an on-board wheelchair when available to move to and from the lavatory.
- To and from the lavatory if you have a mobility problem but are not required to lift or carry you.
- To load and retrieve your carry-on items including mobility aids and other assistive devices stowed on board the aircraft.

Note:

Aircraft personnel are not required to assist you in the lavatory or at your seat in elimination functions.

Aircraft personnel are not required to perform medical services such as the administration of injections.

Foreign Travel

If you are planning travel outside the United States, have your travel agent check if there are accessible facilities in the country or city you wish to visit. Remember that many cities are old. Some countries may not be accessible.

It is imperative that you consider travel health insurance when traveling abroad. Medicare, and many insurance companies with supplemental programs, does not extend its coverage outside the United States.

Have your travel agent check for:

- ☐ Passport requirements

- ☐ Visa requirements
- ☐ Vaccination requirements
- ☐ Rate of money exchange
- ☐ Credit card acceptance
- ☐ Weather and temperature

If you are traveling overseas with a service animal, be sure you know the quarantine regulations of the countries you wish to visit. Obtain all the necessary vaccinations for the return of your service animal to the United States. Information on how to travel with a service animal outside the United States can be obtained from the state or national office of

The United States Department of Agriculture
USDA, APHIS, VS
National Center for Imports & Exports
4700 River Road
Unit 39
Riverdale, Maryland 20737-1231
1-301-734-8590

CHAPTER III

RAIL TRAVEL (USA)

The Americans with Disabilities Act of 1990 has made travel accessible for persons with disabilities. One of the forms of transportation covered by this act is intercity rail travel commonly known as AMTRAK. Although knowing how to travel by rail is important for a person with a disability, preparing to travel is equally important.

Before Traveling

Check with your physician to see if your condition will permit you to travel.

If your physician says that are able to travel, then have your physician give you a written statement concerning your medical condition such as allergies requiring medication, and your current treatment.

Things To Have Before You Travel

- ☐ A copy of your prescriptions in case you should need an emergency refill.
- ☐ Two sets of medication—carry one set with you and the other set in your luggage.
- ☐ Enough medication to last a few days longer than your planned trip.
- ☐ An extra pair of prescription eyeglasses.

- ☐ Your physician's name and phone number in case an emergency should arise while traveling.
- ☐ Extra batteries if you are hearing impaired.

Travel Tips

Decide when you want to travel and where you want to travel, then contact a travel agent and discuss your travel plans. Tell the travel agent the nature of your disability and needs.

Although not required, it is recommended that you have a traveling companion to assist you.

Check the fares. AMTRAK gives a person with a disability a discount on regular fares, but excursion or promotional fares could be lower.

It is advisable to carry a current major credit card.

Make your reservations as far in advance as possible in order to reserve an accessible seat on a coach or an accessible sleeping compartment.

Purchase Amtrak's Trip Protection Insurance to protect your investment in the event you might have to cancel your plans.

Amtrak's Great American Vacation

If your travel includes an air/rail plan, either your travel agent or AMTRAK should inform the assigned air carrier of the nature of your disability and your needs.

> If your AMTRAK GREAT AMERICAN VACATION includes hotels, have AMTRAK check the selected hotels for accessibility according to your disability.

If your travel includes a rail/car rental plan, either your travel agent or AMTRAK should check the car rental company for the availability of an accessible vehicle if such a vehicle is needed.

If your travel includes a rail/motorcoach escorted vacation, your travel agent or AMTRAK should check with the assigned touring company to see if your disability will allow you to participate in the escorted tour.

Denial Of Transportation

You cannot be denied transportation because of your disability whether it is physical, lack of mobility, appearance or involuntary behavior.

However, you can be denied transportation if you engage in violent, seriously disruptive or illegal conduct and pose a threat of danger to the health and safety of the other passengers.

Service Charges

You cannot be charged extra for the provision of services required for your transportation.

For The Wheelchair Passenger

Travel with a portable, folding wheelchair.

Bring extra nuts, bolts and special tools if you have to make repairs to your wheelchair.

Local bicycle shops are a good source if you need replacement parts such as tires and for major repairs.

Boarding Assistance For The Passenger With A Physical Or Mobile Impairment

Boarding assistance will be provided if you are a passenger with mobility impairment or using a wheelchair. A 24-hour advance notice is required.

Wheelchair lifts are available at most major staffed stations. If a lift is not available, manual assistance can be provided. Here again you will have to give advance notice.

Accessible Coach Seating

AMTRAK coaches, both single-level and bi-level, have a limited number of accessible seats for a passenger with mobility problems, with or without a wheelchair, and a place to fold and store a wheelchair. These accessible seats are reserved on a space-available basis. It is recommended that you make your reservation as far in advance as possible. Availability will be guaranteed at the time of reservation and confirmed at the time of sale.

Accessible Sleeping Compartments

There are a limited number of accessible sleeping compartments with direct access restrooms on long-distances trains. If you are using a wheelchair or assistive aids and wish to reserve an accessible sleeping compartment, you should make your reservation as far in advance as possible.

Accessible Restrooms

Accessible restrooms are provided in single-level passenger and food service cars. If your disability prevents your reaching the restroom on your own, you can request assistance from the car attendant.

Dining Car Service

If you are a wheelchair passenger, dining service in a single-level dining car will be provided if you can enter the dining car through an accessible car adjacent to the dining car.

You cannot be denied service because of your disability nor can you be screened from other passengers or be required to sit in a special area of the dining car. You do not have to sit in accessible seats if you do not wish to do so.

On bi-level trains, dining cars are not required to be accessible. Food service will be supplied to you in the lounge. Appropriate aids and services, such as a hard surface to eat on will be provided. If a companion is traveling with you, the same service shall be afforded to him or her.

Food service can also be supplied to you at your seat or sleeping compartment if you are unable to reach the dining car. This service will also be supplied to your traveling companion.

Special Meal Service

If you require special or ethnic foods, you must give AMTRAK 72 hours notice. Have your travel agent call the special service desk to make arrangements.

On-Board Services

On long-distance trains, any assistance needed can be provided by the Car Attendant, Chief of On-Board Services or the Conductor.

On long-distance trains, you can request the Car Attendant provide you with meal or beverage service from the dining car or lounge car. On short-distance trains, the Conductor is able to meet your needs.

You can request that the Conductor or the Car Attendant notify you when near your destination.

TDD/TTY Services For The Hearing Impaired

If transportation information regarding fares and schedules is supplied to the general public via telephone, then the same information shall be supplied to you by a TDD/TTY service if you are hearing impaired.

The Diabetic Traveler

If you are diabetic and require refrigeration for your insulin, it is recommended that you bring an ice cooler. AMTRAK will be glad to furnish the ice. It is recommended that you carry several vials of insulin with you in case of breakage.

The Visually Impaired Traveler

Because of the noise of the train, which can be distracting, it is recommended that you make arrangements with the Car Attendant to escort you to the restroom or dining car. You should never attempt to do this on your own.

Service Animals

You must inform AMTRAK that you are traveling with a service animal.

A service animal may accompany you aboard the train and there is no charge. If your service animal is a guide dog, it must be certified. You are required to have proof of the need of a guide dog and carry proper documentation showing certification. You must control your service animal at all times.

Traveling With An Assistive Device

You are permitted to board with an assistive device such as a ventilator or respirator. Your device must be self-sustained, battery operated, and not rely on train-generated power. You must give AMTRAK advance notice that you will be traveling with an assistive device. There is a weight limit of 75 pounds.

Traveling With Oxygen

You may be required to travel with a companion.

You cannot be charged for the transport of your oxygen system.

It is recommended that you travel with a portable, self-sustained oxygen system.

AMTRAK requires a 12 hour minimum advance notice if you are traveling with an oxygen system. Your travel agent should call the special service desk of AMTRAK.

You will be permitted to board with your oxygen system if it is for medical reasons.

Your equipment must not weigh more than 75 pounds per unit and must be UL or FM listed.

Although it is not mandatory, it is recommended that you reserve a private compartment when traveling with an oxygen system.

You may board with a concentrator, but it must be self-sustained, not dependent on the train-generated power, and have a 12 hour back-up oxygen system.

All wheeled oxygen tanks must have the wheels removed on board the train.

AMTRAK does not supply oxygen on board the train nor in the station. You should bring enough oxygen to last you longer than your scheduled trip.

Before departure:

- Inform your oxygen supplier of your travel plans. Your oxygen supplier can possibly recommend the best system to travel with and make arrangements for oxygen refills at stops and destinations.
- Get the names of suppliers enroute, their location, the refill charges and the form of payment accepted.

Although AMTRAK does not require a prescription from your physician to travel aboard the train with oxygen, you will need a prescription from your physician to obtain refills of oxygen at stops and your destination. The prescription must indicate the liter-per-minute flowrate.

AMTRAK Services

AMTRAK, recognizing that transportation should be available for persons with disabilities, is continuing to improve accessibility of train stations and intercity rail cars. Although most of the improvements are for the wheelchair passenger, the needs of other passengers with disabilities are being addressed.

Boarding Assistance

AMTRAK has wheelchair lifts at many major stations. Where wheelchair lifts are not available, AMTRAK offers manual assistance to board. Advance notice is required in either instance.

At staffed stations, AMTRAK has personnel who will assist the wheelchair passenger or the passenger using mobility aids to board and detrain. AMTRAK requires 24 hour advance notice and arrival at the station one hour before departure.

Amtrak Special Services Desk

AMTRAK offers a special services desk to assist passengers with disabilities in arranging their travel plans. To reach the special services desk, call 1-800-USA-RAIL for passengers with a mobility or visual impairment.

1-800-523-6590 a TDD/TTY service offered for the hearing impaired. This service is offered 24 hours a day, 7 days a week.

Battery-Operated Wheelchairs

Standard-sized battery-operated wheelchairs may be transported in at least one passenger car on most trains.

Bus Connections For The Wheelchair Passenger

Where AMTRAK does not go directly into certain cities, AMTRAK offers connecting bus service. However,

1. A wheelchair passenger must be able to board the bus unassisted.
2. Wheelchairs will be folded and stored on the bus or in the baggage compartment.
3. Passengers with disabilities must occupy a standard seat on the bus.

Accessible Accommodations

Seating

AMTRAK offers accessible coach seating for passengers with disabilities, with or without a wheelchair. As seating space is limited, reservations should be made as far in advance as possible. Availability is guaranteed at the time of booking and confirmed at the time of sale.

Short-Distance Trains

On short-distance trains, AMTRAK has at least one coach with accessible seating. Trains that offer food service have one car with accessible seating.

Long-Distance Trains

On long-distance trains, AMTRAK offers accessible seating and restrooms in the coach.

Where available, AMTRAK has a limited number of accessible sleeping compartments with direct access restrooms on long-distance trains. It is recommended that a passenger with a wheelchair or mobility aid problem reserve a sleeping compartment at the time of booking.

Service Animals

AMTRAK permits certified guide and service animals to accompany a passenger with a disability at no charge. AMTRAK does require proper documentation to prove the need of a service animal.

Assistive Devices

Self-sustained assistive devices such as a respirator, ventilator, or a portable oxygen system are permitted to board with the passenger who has need of such support systems. AMTRAK requires that the life support system be self-sustained and not depend on the train generated electrical power. There is a weight limit.

Special Meal Services

AMTRAK can offer at-seat or in-room food service for passengers with disabilities.

Special menu selections including ethnic, dietetic and low fat/low cholesterol are available on many trains. AMTRAK requires a 72-hour notice before departure to arrange special food requests.

Who To See For On-Board Services

On long-distance trains, assistance can be offered by:

1. The Car Attendant, who can provide meal and beverage service from the dining car or lounge car for passengers with disabilities.
2. The Conductor.
3. The Chief of On-board Services if he or she is available.

CHAPTER IV

BUS TRAVEL (USA)

Intercity bus travel (over-the-road buses) is an inexpensive but often times an uncomfortable way to travel especially for the passenger with a disability. Even the shortest trip can be a trying experience. Before deciding to travel by bus, check out accessibility and comfort. Make sure it is the way you want to travel.

Before Traveling

Consult with your physician to see if your condition will permit you to travel by bus.

If your physician gives his or her consent, then have your physician give you a written statement concerning your medical condition, allergies to medication, and your current treatment.

Things To Have Before You Travel

- ☐ A copy of your prescriptions in case you should need an emergency refill.

- ☐ Two sets of medication, carry one set with you and the other set in your luggage.
- ☐ Enough medication to last a few days longer than your planned trip.
- ☐ An extra pair of prescription eyeglasses.
- ☐ Your physician's name and phone number with you in case you need emergency medical services or prescription refills.
- ☐ Extra batteries if you are hearing impaired.

Travel Tips

Decide when you want to travel and the length of the trip.

Consult with a travel agent. Inform the travel agent of your travel plans, the nature of your disability and your travel needs.

Consider traveling with a companion. Greyhound will permit a companion to travel free to accompany a passenger with a disability. You must have proof of disability either by appearing in person or have a written statement from your physician.

Check the fares so you can determine the best time to travel. Fares could be lower on certain travel days, advance booking or special travel packages.

Carry a major current credit card.

Denial Of Transportation

You cannot be denied transportation on the basis of a physical disability, or because of appearance, or because of involuntary behavior.

However, you can be denied transportation if your disability poses a threat or danger to the health and safety of other passengers.

Designated Seating

You are not required to sit in any designated seats if you do not wish to do so.

Boarding Assistance For The Physically Disabled

You can request assistance to board and disembark if you are physically disabled. If a wheelchair lift is not available, manual assistance may be provided by trained personnel. You are required to give 48 hour advance notice if boarding assistance is needed either by lifting device or manually.

Traveling With A Wheelchair

Travel with a lightweight, folding wheelchair. If possible, your wheelchair can accompany you into the passenger compartment of the bus. The driver or other personnel will assist you in stowing and retrieving your wheelchair. If your wheelchair cannot be accommodated in the passenger compartment of the bus, it will be stowed in the baggage compartment providing that the size of the baggage compartment will accommodate your wheelchair.

If your wheelchair is electric operated, try to equip it with a dry or gel-cell battery. The Department of Transportation rules that a wet-cell battery must be removed from an electric wheelchair and packaged in a leak proof container or covered with spill proof caps if your wheelchair cannot be transported in an upright position in the baggage compartment.

You should bring extra nuts, bolts, and special tools in the event you may have to dismantle or repair your wheelchair.

Local bicycle shops can be a good source for spare parts and major repairs if you have need of such services away from home.

You are not required to sign a waiver of liability for the loss or damage to your wheelchair.

On-Board Restrooms

Restrooms on the bus are inaccessible for the wheelchair passenger. You should use the restrooms at the bus depot before departure for comfort and convenience. Also use the restroom at any bus stops.

The Hearing Impaired Traveler

If you have a hearing impairment, you can request a TDD/TTY service for information about transportation and services if such a service is supplied to the general public via telephone.

On-Board Assistance For The Visually Impaired Traveler

All transfer points, major intersections, destination points and intervals along the route shall be announced. You may request the announcement of a particular stop.

Assistance will be provided if it is necessary to make a connection with another bus or any other form of transportation at a transfer point.

Traveling With An Assistive Device

You will be allowed to board at no extra charge with an assistive device such as a ventilator or respirator. Your assistive device must be self-sustained. It is recommended that you use dry or gel-cell batteries. The driver or personnel will assist you in boarding and helping in the stowing and retrieving of your assistive device.

Traveling With A Service Animal

You must notify the bus carrier that you are traveling with a service animal.

A certified dog shall accompany you in the passenger compartment of the bus free of charge. You should have proper documentation to prove the need of a guide dog and show its certification. You are required to control your service animal at all times either by harness, muzzle, leash or verbal commands. Your guide dog will be allowed to accompany you to your seat but must not obstruct the aisle.

Traveling With Oxygen

Travel with a portable self-sustained oxygen system.

You are permitted to board with three tanks of oxygen. Your tanks are required to accompany you to your seat, fit under your feet, and not obstruct the aisle.

It is your responsibility to make arrangements to have your tank refilled enroute to your destination. Before departure, you should notify your oxygen supplier of your itinerary so that your supplier can arrange for some one to meet you with oxygen. You should have a list of oxygen suppliers, their locations, refill charges and accepted form of payment.

You will need a prescription from your physician to show the need for oxygen in order to obtain refills. The prescription should indicate the liter-per-minute flow.

If possible, you should carry enough oxygen to last the duration of the trip.

If it is necessary to transport your tanks in the baggage compartment of the bus, they must be emptied. Filled oxygen tanks are not permitted to be transported in the baggage compartment as per Department of Transportation rules.

The Diabetic Traveler

If you are diabetic, bring a small cooler packed with ice to refrigerate your insulin. Carry extra vials of insulin with you in case of breakage.

Special Foods

Special dietetic and ethnic foods are your responsibility while traveling aboard the bus. Be sure to pack whatever foods you might need.

Greyhound Services

The Greyhound Lines, Inc. provides special services to make bus travel for persons with disabilities accessible and comfortable.

Special Services Desk

Greyhound offers a special services desk for persons with disabilities.

Call 1-800-752-4841 for the passenger traveling alone.

Call 1-800-231-2222 for the passenger with a companion.

Call 1-800-345-3109 (TDD) for the hearing impaired.

Traveling With A Companion

Greyhound will allow a passenger with a disability to travel alone providing the passenger can tend to his or her personal needs and can remain in a seat.

If a traveling companion is required, Greyhound will allow the companion to travel free of charge. Proof of a passenger's disability is required either by appearing in person or having a written statement from a physician.

Boarding Assistance

In order to provide assistance to a passenger with a disability, Greyhound requires 48 hours notice before departure. The passenger should supply his or her itinerary and travel needs.

Greyhound will notify the Customer Service personnel of the passenger's itinerary and special needs at the point of departure, transfer points, final destination and any connecting carriers involved in the routing.

Wheelchair And Assistive Devices

Greyhound will stow a passenger's wheelchair or assistive devices in the passenger compartment of the bus, if possible, or in the baggage compartment at no extra cost. An electrically operated wheelchair will have its battery removed and stored in accordance with the Department of Transportation rules on transporting hazardous materials.

Boarding And Disembarking

The driver or other personnel will assist a passenger with a disability to board or disembark. Also the driver will assist in the stowage and retrieval of assistive devices. However, it is not required that the driver hand carry a passenger with a disability on board the bus. It is the driver's discretion to assist in hand carrying a passenger on board but the driver must be trained in assisting a passenger with a disability to board or disembark.

Service Animals

Greyhound will permit a service animal to accompany a passenger with a disability in the passenger compartment of the bus. Greyhound will require proof of the need for a service animal and its certification is required. The passenger must keep the service animal under control at all times.

~~

CHAPTER V

RENTING A VEHICLE (USA)

Renting a vehicle is the only form of transportation which offers freedom and independence. You are free to go where you want and when you want. And, you have the feeling of independence in which you are able to make your own decisions and not have to rely on anyone to provide transportation. Even a person with a disability can enjoy these same privileges, although with limitations. For a person with a disability, renting a vehicle requires knowledge, planning and preparation.

Before Traveling

Before deciding to rent a vehicle and travel, check with your physician to see if you are physically fit to travel.

If your physician consents, have him or her give you a written statement concerning your medical condition, allergies, and medical treatment.

Things To Have Before You Travel

- ☐ A copy of your prescriptions in case an emergency refill is needed.
- ☐ Two sets of medication—carry one set with you and one set in your luggage.
- ☐ Enough medication to last the entire trip.
- ☐ A spare pair of prescription eyeglasses.
- ☐ Your physician's name and phone number in case you should need advice in an medical emergency.
- ☐ Extra batteries if you are hearing impaired.

Travel Tips

Air/Drive Travel

If you are planning to fly to your destination and rent a car, either you or your travel agent should inform the air carrier the nature of your disability and needs. Knowing how to travel is just as important as knowing how to rent a car.

If you are purchasing a land/air package, ask if a rental car is included. If a rental car is not included, find out if you can rent a car at a special rate.

Traveling With A Companion

Consider traveling with a companion to assist you in driving and with your personal needs.

If you are traveling with a companion, both you and your companion should be licensed drivers.

Credit Card Requirement

You should possess a current major credit card. All car rental agencies, domestic and foreign, require a current credit card to guarantee deposit, full payment and any collision claims.

Special Diets

If you require special foods or beverages while driving, be sure to pack your needed items in a cooler.

Handicap Identification

Carry the international handicap logo with you and place it on the rear view mirror. This will identify you as a person with a disability and permit you to park in spaces reserved for people with a disability.

Communication

If you can, carry a cellular phone with you. This will enable you to call for road service or the local police at 911 if you have a flat tire, mechanical problem or other emergencies.

When To Reserve A Vehicle

If you are planning to travel during holidays or peak season, you should consider reserving your vehicle as far in advance as possible of your travel date. The size and type of vehicle you want might not be available with a last minute booking.

The Hearing Impaired Traveler

A driver with a hearing impairment should carry a hearing impaired sticker whether it is a rental car or a rented accessible van.

The Diabetic Traveler

Carry a small cooler packed with ice to refrigerate your insulin and several extra vials of insulin in case of breakage.

The Wheelchair Traveler

Consider traveling with a lightweight, collapsible wheelchair for ease of handling and stowage. Battery operated wheelchairs may require an accessible van with a wheelchair lift and battery operated wheelchairs have a tendency to be cumbersome.

The Traveler Using Oxygen

Avoid high altitudes.

Travel with a portable oxygen system.

Before departing, have your travel agent check to see what the requirements are for traveling with oxygen by air, rail or bus to a destination and then renting a car.

In your rental car, ask the other passengers not to smoke.

Your oxygen tanks should be securely fastened and a window must always be left open a crack to prevent an oxygen build up in the car.

If you are using a liquid system, it must be kept in an upright position. Do not store a liquid unit in the trunk of a car.

If you have the need for oxygen on the trip, notify your oxygen supplier of your travel plans. Your oxygen supplier will determine the best system to use, how much oxygen to take and will contact other suppliers for oxygen enroute and at your destination.

Have your physician give you a prescription to show the need for oxygen and the liter flow rate. You will need the prescription to prove the need of oxygen to a supplier to obtain refills.

Before you travel, you should have the names and locations of oxygen suppliers, the refill charge, and the form of payment accepted.

Try to have an adequate supply of oxygen in the vehicle.

Renting A Car

Decide what type, size and how long you want to rent a car. Rental rates are based on

- Size of car
- Type of car
- Daily, weekly or weekend rental
- Mileage caps
- Holiday or peak season

Instead of calling several car rental agencies to check availability, it is recommended that you contact a travel agent who will have a listing of car rental agencies, availability and rental rates that can be accessed through the office computer.

Inform the travel agent:

- The type and size of car you want.
- When you want to pick up the car.
- Where you will pick up the car.
- How long you want to rent it.

If you have a physical disability, try to rent the biggest car you can afford for greater comfort and convenience. Do not let price be the determining factor. For a person who is traveling with a wheelchair, it is recommended that a minivan be considered. Most car rental agencies will have minivans for rent.

If needed, ask for a car with right or left hand controls. It is recommended that you reserve a hand control vehicle far in advance of your travel date as there is a limited supply of these vehicles. Twenty-four-hour advance notice is required to rent a hand control vehicle and have it delivered to a given location.

Be sure to check if there is a drop-off charge for a one-way car rental and which location offers the lowest car rental rate - airport or city.

Insurance Coverage

Check with your insurance agent to see if your automobile policy covers rental vehicles. If you are not covered, then consider adding a rider.

If you do not have insurance coverage, you will be required to purchase "COLLISION DAMAGE WAIVER" from the car rental agency which will increase your rental rate.

Check with your insurance agent to see if your homeowner's policy covers loss or damage to your wheelchair.

Renting An Accessible Van

There are a number of national companies that specialize in renting accessible vans. There are two ways for you to rent an accessible van. Either drive the van yourself or have the rental company supply the driver. The rates will be based on:

- If you do the driving.
- If a driver is supplied.
- Daily or weekly rates.

- One way or round trip travel.

Before renting an accessible van, either you or your travel agent should ask the following questions. The answers you will receive will determine if renting an accessible van is for you.

Questions To Ask

- What is the rental rate if you drive or if a driver is supplied?
- What is the daily or weekly rate?
- Is insurance necessary?
- What are the one-way and round trip rates?
- What is the mileage cap and the rate per mile over the cap?
- What is the drop-off charge if you pick up your vehicle in one city and leave it in another city?
- Does the van have removable seats?
- Are tie downs provided for wheelchairs?
- Is the van equipped with an automatic wheelchair lift?
- Is the van air conditioned?
- Is there room for several passengers and luggage?
- Can the van be delivered to a given destination?

If you are planning to travel, try to reserve your accessible van well in advance of your travel date. There is a limited supply of such vehicles and they might not be available during the peak travel season or holidays.

Local Automobile Dealers

There are also local dealers that rent accessible vans in several cities and tourist regions of the country. To find a dealer, look in the Yellow Pages under:

- Automotive - Handicapped
- Automotive - Disabled Equipped
- Disabled Persons Transportation Service

The same questions should be asked of a local dealer as those asked of a national dealer in regards to renting an accessible van.

The Americans With Disabilities Act

The Americans with Disabilities Act of 1990 defines what automobile rental agencies must do in making facilities accessible for persons with a disability.

Accessibility To Service

One entrance to the agency's rental office is required to be accessible, preferably the main entrance.

Guide dogs are allowed to accompany a customer with a visual impairment into the rental office.

Traveling In Comfort

Wear loose and comfortable clothing.

Don't lace your shoes too tight as feet have a tendency to swell due to inactivity.

Don't try to travel too long each day.

Every several hours, take a rest stop and stretch your legs.

Make your hotel or motel reservations ahead of time.

Reconfirm your reservations at each overnight stop.

Service cannot be denied to a person with a disability even if the disability may be disturbing to others.

Service For The Hearing Impaired

Automotive rental agencies are not required to have a TDD service for the hearing impaired.

A sign language interpreter is not necessary for the hearing impaired customer. Communication by writing notes, word board or lip reading is considered effective.

For The Customer With A Speech Impediment

An automotive rental agency should allow sufficient time for a person with such a disability to express himself of herself or read a message spelled out on a word board.

Shuttle Service

If the rental agency provides shuttle transportation to a lot where vehicles for rent are located for its customers, then the same service must be provided to persons with a disability.

Hand Control Vehicles

A car rental office is required to install vehicle hand controls if it is readily achievable. Readily achievable means without great difficulty or expense.

Credit Card Acceptance

The credit card of the customer with a disability who is not the driver and who has arranged for someone else to drive, must be accepted.

A Few General Considerations When Traveling...

Cancellation Insurance

Consider purchasing cancellation insurance. Regardless of your mode of transportation, the small cost of insurance will be more than offset if an emergency should arise and you want to get your payment back. You have a choice. You can spend $3000.00 on a cruise and protect your investment or lose the full amount if forced to cancel by not having any type of cancellation insurance. This also applies to the purchase of airline, rail or bus tickets.

Medical Insurance

Check medical insurance for coverage outside the USA. Medicare and many insurance companies do not extend coverage outside the USA. Purchasing medical insurance with your cancellation insurance could help defray the cost of medical treatment.

CHAPTER VI

TAKING A TOUR (USA)

One of the most popular ways for sightseeing is to take a planned motorcoach tour. Everything is included in the tour—transportation, meals, hotel or motel accommodations, visiting historic sights, and entertainment. Is touring for everyone? Can a person with a disability enjoy the pleasures of touring? The answer lies with you, the person with a disability.

Before Taking A Tour

Before you decide to take a tour, contact your physician to see if you are physically fit to travel.

If your physician approves, then have your physician give you a written statement concerning your medical condition, allergies and current treatment.

Things To Have Before Taking A Tour

- ☐ Copies of your prescriptions in case of emergency refills.

- ☐ Two sets of medication. Carry one set with you and one set in your luggage.
- ☐ Your physician's name and phone number if a medical emergency should arise or if you need an emergency prescription refill.
- ☐ Medication to last longer than the tour.
- ☐ An extra pair of prescription eyeglasses.
- ☐ Extra batteries if you are hearing impaired.

Travel Tips

If your physician consents to you taking a tour, contact a travel agent. Together, you and the travel agent can go over the many brochures to see what tour meets your desires and needs.

The travel agent then can call the tour operator and inform him or her of your tour selection and of your disability. The travel agent should check for accessibility by asking the tour operator the following questions so that you may determine if you should take the tour:

- Is a companion required?
- Can one travel with a wheelchair?
- Is the bus equipped with a wheelchair lift?
- Are the hotels, motels or resorts listed in the brochure accessible to persons with disabilities?
- Are the destinations and sightseeing tours listed in the brochure accessible for the physically disabled?
- Are signers provided for the hearing impaired passenger?
- Are there talking guides for the visually impaired?
- Are the restaurants and dining facilities accessible to persons with disabilities?

- Can arrangements be made for the use a respirator?
- Can accommodations be made for the use of a portable oxygen system?
- Can a certified guide dog be allowed to accompany a passenger who has need of a guide dog?

The tour operator will inform the travel agent if you will be allowed to participate in the tour because of your disability. A tour operator has the right to accept or reject any person as a tour participant.

If You Are Accepted

- ...and the tour includes **air travel**, have your travel agent or tour operator inform the assigned air carrier the nature of your disability and travel needs.
- ...and the tour includes **rail travel**. have your travel agent or tour operator check the rail company for accessibility.
- ...and the tour includes a **cruise**, have your travel agent or tour operator check to see if there are accessible facilities on board the ship.
- ...and the tour consists of travel by **motorcoach, air, rail and cruise**, make sure that all forms of transportation are accessible to persons with disabilities in order for you to enjoy every phase of the tour.
- Purchase low-cost accident, sickness, baggage, and trip cancellation insurance to protect your investment. The cost of this insurance will more than offset the price if you have to cancel your tour in the event of emergency. Your travel agent should have the necessary forms to purchase insurance.

- Use the restroom before departure and at any rest stops. On-board restrooms on motorcoaches are not accessible for the wheelchair participant.
- Wear light and loose clothing while traveling. Do not tie your shoes too tightly as feet have a tendency to swell due to inactivity.
- Don't forget to carry your medication with you.
- Consider traveling with a companion to assist you in all your needs.
- Carry a current major credit card.

Specialized Tour Operators

There are a number of tour operators that specialize in arranging tours for persons with a disability. The names of these tour operators and the type of tours they offer can be found in the OFFICIAL TOUR DIRECTORY. This directory should be found in your travel agent's office.

By using a specialized tour operator, you can eliminate all the hassle of arranging a tour. The only thing you have to do is to pick a tour operator whose service will cater to your particular disability.

Although these tours may be more expensive than a regular tour, the benefits of having everything arranged for you will far outweigh the cost.

How To Tour With A Disability

If you are permitted to participate in a tour, you should know how to travel depending on your disability.

For The Wheelchair Passenger

Travel with a lightweight, folding wheelchair for ease of transportation and stowage.

Bring extra nuts, bolts and special tools if it is necessary to dismantle or repair your wheelchair.

If you should need spare parts while touring, local bicycle shops are a good source.

For The Diabetic Passenger

Travel with a small cooler packed with ice to refrigerate your insulin and carry several vials of insulin in case of breakage.

Traveling With Oxygen

If you have a respiratory problem and require oxygen, travel with a portable self-sustained oxygen system. It is your responsibility to see to the refill of your oxygen tanks. Before departure, you should inform your oxygen supplier of your itinerary. Your supplier will advise you on the best oxygen system to travel with and arrange for someone to meet you at stops and at your destination. You should also have the names of oxygen suppliers and their locations as well as the refill charges and form of payment. You will need a prescription from your physician to show the need for oxygen and the liter-per-minute flow rate in order to obtain refills.

For The Visually Impaired Traveler

If you need the services of a guide dog, have your travel agent inquire of the tour company what the requirements are for touring with a guide dog.

The Hearing Impaired Traveler

Travel with a companion who can assist you in understanding and explaining the various sights and lectures on the tour. Tour companies are not required to provide signers on the tour.

Tour Operators' Terms & Conditions

A tour operator reserves the right to accept or reject any person as a tour participant.

Any disability requiring special attention should be reported at the time the reservation is made. A tour operator will make reasonable attempts to accommodate the special needs of disabled tour participants, but is not responsible for any denial of services by carriers, hotels, restaurants, and other independent suppliers. Bus company and other carrier employees an representatives may not physically lift participants or assist them on or off transportation vehicles. Persons requiring such assistance must be accompanied by a qualified companion.

Tour membership is available to all travelers and will not be withheld if the tour operator can furnish special requirements which an individual may need. Should meeting these requirements materially add to the tour operator's cost, the individual would be expected to pay these additional costs.

A tour director retains the right to terminate the membership of any tour member if any physical or mental disability becomes disruptive while on the tour and causes hardship to the tour director and/or other tour members.

A tour operator reserves the right to expel from the tour any participant whose conduct is deemed incompatible with the interests of the tour group.

A tour operator reserves the right to terminate the tour of any persons who are abusive of others or whose behavior otherwise disrupts the operation of the tour.

A tour operator reserves the right not to accept or retain anyone on tour whose condition or general deportment impedes the operation of the tour or affects the rights of other passengers.

A tour operator cannot provide individual assistance to a tour member for walking, dining or other personal needs.

Tour participants who require any form of personal assistance must be accompanied by a companion who is capable of, and totally responsible for providing such assistance.

Persons with severe dietary restrictions must be advised that special diet orders cannot be accommodated.

CHAPTER VII

ACCOMMODATIONS

HOTELS, MOTELS, RESORTS (USA)

Whether you are planning to stay at a hotel, motel or resort, locally, on a trip or on a vacation, the basic service they all offer is lodging. For a person without a disability, selecting a destination and making a reservation is simple. Either you, or your travel agent can call your chosen destination and make a reservation. But for a person with a disability, this is the most difficult part in arranging a trip or vacation. Each person's disability is different, and each person's needs are different. Only by careful research and planning can you determine if the destination you have chosen fits your needs. Do not accept the fact that when a hotel, motel or resort advertises it is accessible that it is accessible. You must check and recheck to be sure that it is *usable* as well as accessible.

Before Traveling

Check with your physician to see if you are physically fit to travel.

If your physician gives his or her consent, then have your physician give you a written statement concerning your medical condition, allergies, and current treatment.

Things To Have Before You Travel

- ☐ A copy of your prescriptions with you in case you should need an emergency refill.
- ☐ Two sets of medication. Carry one set with you and one set in your luggage.
- ☐ Your physician's name and phone number in case of a medical emergency or the need of an emergency prescription refill.
- ☐ A spare pair of prescription eyeglasses.
- ☐ A current major credit card.
- ☐ Extra batteries if you are hearing impaired.

How To Travel With A Disability

Knowing how to travel with a disability by plane, train, bus or drive is just as important as selecting the right destination.

For The Wheelchair Traveler

Travel with a lightweight, collapsible wheelchair for ease of handling and stowage. Battery operated wheelchairs can be cumbersome and difficult to maneuver. There are restrictions when traveling with a wheelchair by air, train or bus whether your wheelchair is folding or electric. Before making a reservation, you should check what the restrictions are for the transportation you have chosen.

Traveling With Oxygen

It is recommended that you travel with a portable, self-sustained oxygen system. Before departure, either you or your travel agent should inquire about restrictions on traveling with oxygen for the form of transportation that you have chosen.

You should inform your oxygen supplier of your travel plans. Your supplier will recommend the right system for travel and make arrangements for someone to meet you with oxygen refills at stops and at your destination.

You must have a prescription from your physician, preferably in triplicate, showing your need of oxygen and the liter-per-minute flow rate.

Before departure, you should get the names of oxygen suppliers, their location, the refill charges and the form of payment accepted.

For The Diabetic Traveler

Depending on your form of transportation, consider traveling with a small cooler packed with ice to refrigerate your insulin. Carry extra vials of insulin in case of breakage.

Traveling With A Service Animal

You must inform the carrier of your choice and the destination that you have selected that you are traveling with a service animal. If your service animal is a guide dog, you must have proper documentation to prove that the guide dog is certified. You must also control your guide dog by harness, leash, muzzle or verbal command at all times.

Travel Tips

Consider traveling with a companion.

Decide where you want to go on vacation and when you want to go.

Contact a travel agent who will have brochures with hotels, motels, resorts and destinations. Together, you and your travel agent can select the destination that most appeals to you.

Inform the travel agent of the nature of your disability and your needs. The travel agent can then inquire about services offered and special accommodations for your particular disability, and get the best rates available.

Before Making A Reservation

For The Wheelchair Guest

ASK:

- Is the room and bathroom accessible and usable? The bathroom may be accessible but may not be usable if you need a roll-in shower.
- Is the room large enough for you to move around comfortably in a wheelchair?
- Is the room accessible according to your disability? The accommodation will do you no good if it is accessible for a person who is in a wheelchair and you are visually impaired.
- Are other amenities, such as restaurants, lounges and pools, accessible to people with your disability?

For The Visually Impaired Guest

ASK:

- Can an audio cassette be sent to you describing the features of the facility?
- Are there Braille or large print menus?
- Is there Braille signage on elevator doors?
- Are there raised numbers on the room doors?
- Is there a vibrating pillow or bed to inform you of incoming phone calls?
- Is there a talking or vibrating alarm clock?
- Can a qualified reader be supplied if one is needed?

For The Hearing Impaired Guest

ASK:

- Are there are devices such as flashing lights to alert you visually if the phone rings if there is a knock at the door or if there is an emergency?
- Is there a vibrating pillow or vibrating bed to alert you to incoming phone calls?
- Is there an alarm device to awaken you in the morning?
- Can a signer be provided by the facility if a signer is needed?
- Are there closed captioned decoders on the room televisions?

Note:

Auxiliary aids and devices for individuals with hearing or speech or vision impairments must be provided unless providing such auxiliary aids and devices would result in an undue burden, such as a difficulty or expense, or alter the delivery of services.

However a public accommodation must offer another means of auxiliary aid, if it is available, and the alternate means does not result in a fundamental alteration or undue burden.

Service animals must be permitted at no charge although advance authorization may be required.

Making A Reservation

When making a reservation by phone, get the name of the person taking your reservation in case a problem should arise when checking in.

Request the lowest floor with accessible rooms.

Inform the facility if you are traveling with a guide dog. Get the name of the person you are talking to in case you may have to confirm that you advised the facility about your guide dog.

Ask if all the features of the facility are accessible.

Check and double check that the accommodations meet your needs. The general public usually thinks of a person with a disability as being in a wheelchair, not thinking that there are other disabilities.

Checking In

For The Wheelchair Guest

Check your room and bathroom to see if both are accessible and usable and that the room is large enough to move a wheelchair around comfortably.

For The Visually Impaired Guest

Ask if someone will give you a tour of the facility.

Ask the bellhop to escort you to your room and describe the various temperature controls and their locations and familiarize you with the faucets in the bathroom.

Place a rubber band around important door knobs for ease of identification.

For The Hearing Impaired Guest

Check to see if the aids and devices that you inquired about are provided. If not, then request that they be offered. Bear in mind that places of public accommodation are only required to supply these services if it does not prove to be an undue burden or result in a fundamental alteration. Undue burden means without much difficulty or expense.

Discrimination Is Illegal

You cannot be discriminated against because of your disability whether it is physical, lack of mobility, visual or involuntary behavior.

Denial Of Services

You cannot be denied services or benefits because of your disability.

The ADA Prohibits Discrimination

Title III of the Americans with Disabilities Act of 1990 prohibits discrimination against any individual with a disability.

The Act reads:

A public accommodation may not discriminate against an individual in the operation of a place of public accommodation.

Public accommodations include places of lodging (inns, hotels, motels) except for owner-occupied establishments renting fewer than 6 rooms.

Direct Threat

A hotel, motel or resort may deny you services and benefits if your disability poses a provable threat to the health and safety of the other guests.

Right To Refuse

You are not required to accept different or separate services or benefits if you do not choose to do so.

Equal Benefits

A hotel, motel or resort must provide you with services and benefits that are equal to the services and benefits offered to other guests.

Separate Benefits

You cannot be provided with services and benefits that are different from those provided to other guests. Different or separate services and benefits can only be provided if it is necessary for you to receive the same level of services and benefits offered to other guests.

Integrated Settings

You shall be provided with services and benefits in the most integrated setting appropriate to your needs.

Screening

You cannot be screened from other guests because of your disability even though your disability may be disturbing to others.

Personal Aids And Services

A hotel, motel or resort is not required to provide you personal aids or devices such as wheelchairs, prescription eyeglasses, or hearing aids, or assist you in eating, toiletry, or dressing.

Surcharge

You cannot be assessed a surcharge to cover the costs of measures such as auxiliary aids, and barrier removal.

Service Animals

You are permitted to have a service animal accompany you in a public accommodation. You are responsible for the care and supervision of your service animal.

Auxiliary Aids And Devices

This section applies only to those persons who have a hearing, visual or speech impairment. You cannot be excluded, denied services, segregated, or treated differently from other guests because of the absence of auxiliary aids or services unless it can be demonstrated that providing these services would alter the nature of the facility or result in an undue burden such as significant difficulty or expense. If the provision of auxiliary aids and services results in an undue burden, then alternate auxiliary aids and services shall be provided unless it too causes an undue burden.

Removal Of Barriers

A hotel, motel or resort is required to remove architectural and communicative barriers in existing facilities, unless it can be proved that removing these barriers is not readily accomplishable and able to be carried out without much difficulty or expense.

Elevator Exemption

A hotel, motel or resort is not required to have an elevator if the facility is less than three stories or less than 3000 square feet per story.

CHAPTER VIII

DINING OUT (USA)

We Americans delight in eating out, whether at a fast food place such as Burger King or elegant dining at the Ritz Carlton. But is dining out for everyone? Can a person with a disability enjoy the same dining experience as a person without a disability? The answer is a qualified YES.

Check Accessibility

Never assume that a dining establishment is accessible to persons with disabilities even though it advertises that it is accessible. It is recommended that you check the dining facility and ask if the dining area is accessible to persons with disabilities and usable.

Under the "readily achievable" section of the ADA, a facility need not make a dining room accessible to persons with disabilities if it is too difficult or expensive or disrupts the daily operation of the dining room. However, the facility must provide an alternate method of serving if that method is easily achievable.

When making a reservation at a particular dining establishment, you should check accessibility asking the following questions:

For The Wheelchair Guest

ASK:

- Are there steps at the main entrance?
- If there are steps, how will you gain admission?
- Must you be hand carried or use an alternate means of entrance such as through the kitchen?
- Is the restroom accessible and usable?
- Can the dining area accommodate a wheelchair?

For The Visually Impaired Guest

ASK:

- Are there Braille or large print menus?
- Will someone assist you in ordering?
- Is a service animal permitted?

For The Hearing Impaired Guest

Ask if there is menu board or whether someone will assist you in ordering.

For The Guest With A Respiratory Problem

Ask if there is a no smoking section.

The Americans With Disabilities Act

Title III of the Americans with Disabilities Act of 1990 prohibits discrimination on the basis of disability by a place of public accommodation. An establishment such as a restaurant or bar that serves food and drinks is covered.

Your Rights

- You cannot be denied service because of your disability whether it is a physical disability which requires the use of a wheelchair, or because of appearance such as with Down's Syndrome, or because of involuntary behavior as caused by Cerebral Palsy.
- You cannot be placed in a dining area that is separate or segregated from the normal dining area.
- You cannot be screened because of appearance from the rest of the patrons.
- You are not required to accept service in a designated area if you do not wish to do so.
- You cannot be charged a surcharge for extra services, such as a interpreter.
- You are permitted to be accompanied by a controlled service animal into the dining area.

A Dining Facility's Rights

A dining facility:

- can deny you admission or service if your disability poses a threat or danger to the health and safety of other patrons.

- does not have to provide special devices such as a wheelchair.
- does not have to provide Braille or large print menus if the dining personnel can read the menu to you.
- does not have to provide an interpreter or signer if the menu can be displayed or you are shown the daily specials on a notepad.
- does not have to assist you in feeding or personal hygiene.
- is not required to have a TDD service.

Not all entrances have to be accessible, but the main entrance must be accessible either directly or by use of a ramp and the entrance must have proper lighting.

Not all dining areas have to be accessible if the dining facility has various levels of dining. Only one level area shall be accessible for the same service provided to the general public.

CHAPTER IX

RIVER CRUISING (USA)

River cruising, also known as steamboating, is a unique form of adventure. You are able to return to the Old South and visit the plantations of yesterday, see the Run for the Roses at the Kentucky Derby, pass through the Alton Locks on the way to Minneapolis, and cruise on American waters, be served by an American crew and dine on American food.

You, the person with a disability, can share in this adventure. There is a company that cruises the inland waters of America and welcomes passengers with a disability.

The Delta Queen Steamboat Co.

The Delta Queen Steamboat Company has two boats that have accessible cabins.

The Mississippi Queen has one cabin.

The American Queen has nine cabins.

The boat named the Delta Queen does not have accessible cabins.

Delta Queen Steamboat Company welcomes

- The wheelchair passenger.
- The hearing impaired passenger.
- The visual or sight impaired passenger.

Passengers with a visual or sight impairment are permitted to travel with a service animal or guide dog. The passenger must provide documentation to show certification of the guide dog. The passenger is responsible for the care and supervision of his or her guide dog.

The Delta Queen Steamboat Company will arrange accessible transportation for a wheelchair passenger to participate in side trips. Advance notice is required to arrange accessible transportation at ports of call. The Delta Queen Steamboat Company cannot guarantee that every side trip will be accessible for the wheelchair passenger.

The Delta Queen Steamboat Company recommends that a person with a disability be accompanied by an able-bodied companion.

Before Taking A River Cruise

Check with your physician to see if your condition will permit you to travel and cruise. If your physician consents, have your physician give you a written statement concerning your medical condition, allergies to medication and your current treatment.

Things To Have Before Taking A Cruise

- ☐ A copy of your prescriptions from your physician in case you need an emergency refill.
- ☐ Two sets of medication. Carry one set with you and one in your luggage.
- ☐ Your physician's name and phone number in case of a medical emergency or for the need of an emergency prescription refill.
- ☐ A spare pair of prescription eyeglasses.
- ☐ Extra batteries if you are hearing impaired.

Travel Tips

Before deciding to take a river cruise, consider a traveling companion to assist you in traveling and aboard the steamboat.

Carry a current major credit card.

Purchase low-cost accident, sickness, baggage, and trip cancellation insurance to protect your investment. The cost of this insurance will more than offset the price if you have to cancel your tour in the event of emergency. Your travel agent should have the necessary forms to purchase insurance.

Decide when you want to cruise. You must contact a travel agent to make a reservation. The Delta Queen Steamboat Company only books cruises through travel agents.

Your travel agent will have the Delta Queen Steamboat Company brochure describing the variety of cruises offered. Together, you and your travel agent can select a cruise, the length of the cruise and the sailing package.

If the cruise you have selected is a steamboat plus air package, either your travel agent or the Delta Queen Steamboat Company should tell the air carrier the nature of your disability and your needs.

After selecting a cruise, your travel agent will inform the Delta Queen Steamboat Company of your selected itinerary, describe the nature of your disability and check for the availability of accessible cabins for the time you wish to cruise.

Know How To Travel

Knowing how to travel with a disability by plane, train or bus to your port of embarkation is just as important as selecting the right cruise. Each form of transportation has its own restriction in providing transportation for persons with a disability. Your travel agent should inquire about restrictions that apply to your disability.

> ***Note:***
>
> It is not necessary to have all rooms accessible to persons with disabilities, but a reasonable number of rooms, parking spaces and bathrooms must be accessible.
>
> All amenities such as lounges and swimming pools must be made available to individuals with a disability if they are offered to other individuals who do not have a disability.
>
> Elevators are not required if the facility is under three stories and less than 3000 square feet per story.

The Wheelchair Traveler

Travel with a lightweight, folding wheelchair for ease of handling, mobility and stowage. Battery operated wheelchairs tend to be cumbersome and difficult to maneuver.

Traveling With Oxygen

The Delta Queen Steamboat Company does not provide oxygen on board the boat. You are responsible for making all arrangements when traveling with an oxygen system.

Travel with a portable, self-sustained oxygen system. Inform your oxygen supplier of your travel plans and cruising itinerary. Your oxygen supplier will recommend the best system to travel with and can make arrangements for oxygen refill at stops, ports of call and at your destination.

Get a prescription from your physician indicating your need of oxygen and the liter-per-minute flow.

Before departure, get the names of oxygen suppliers enroute, their locations, refill charges and the accepted form of payment.

The Diabetic Traveler

Consider traveling with a small cooler packed with ice to refrigerate your insulin. Carry extra vials of insulin in case of breakage.

For The Wheelchair Passenger

ASK:

- Are accessible cabins available?
- Where are those cabins located on the boat?
- Are special boarding arrangements necessary?
- Are the bathrooms accessible and usable?
- Can accessible transportation be arranged for side trips?

For The Visually Impaired Passenger

ASK:

- Can an audio cassette be sent to you prior to embarkation so that you will be familiar with the boat's environment?
- Are Braille or large print menus are available?

- Are there auxiliary aids and devices in the cabin:
    - Vibrating pillows or beds are available to alert you to incoming phone calls?
    - A talking or vibrating alarm clock?
    - Raised numbers on the cabin door for identification?
    - Will someone escort you to your cabin, describe the location of the various controls, the placement of the TV and the layout of the bathroom?

For The Hearing Impaired Passenger

ASK:

- Can a signer can be provided so that you can enjoy the lectures?
- Can a video cassette be sent to you prior to embarkation?
- Are there auxiliary aids and devices in the cabin?
    - Flashing lights to alert you to phone calls?
    - A vibrating bed or pillow?
    - Closed and open caption TV?
    - Closed captioned decoders?
- How will you be informed of morning awakenings or the approach of ports of call?

The Americans With Disabilities Act

Accessibility Is Required By Law

Steamboats that cruise American waters come under two sections of the Americans with Disabilities Act of 1990, transportation and accommodation. Steamboats must make travel accessible for persons with a disability.

Your Rights

You cannot be denied boarding because of your disability whether it is a physical impairment which requires you to use a wheelchair, or because of appearance as with Down's Syndrome or because of involuntarily behavior such as that caused by Cerebral Palsy.

You cannot be placed in a separate or segregated environment or screened from other passengers in the dining area.

You are permitted to board with a service animal if a service animal is required. You should have documentation to prove the need of a service animal.

You are not required to sit in a designated area in the dining room nor accept special accessible accommodations if you do not wish to.

Steamboat Company Rights

Steamboat Companies have the right to deny you boarding if your disability poses a threat or danger to the health and safety of other passengers.

CHAPTER X

OCEAN CRUISING

In the world of travel, ocean cruising has become one of the most popular and exciting forms of vacationing. Although many of the cruise ships are of foreign registry and do not come under the Americans with Disabilities Act of 1990, cruise lines are beginning to realize that cruising is for everyone. Cruise lines are providing accessible cabins on their newer ships and refitting their older ships to accommodate passengers with a disability. But all is not perfect. Embarking and debarking is still a problem. Access to all areas of the ship is still a problem. Participating in island tours is still a problem. But even with these weaknesses, it should not deter you from taking a cruise.

Before Taking A Cruise

Check with your physician to see if your condition will permit you to travel and cruise.

If your physician gives his or her permission, then get a statement from your physician concerning your medical condition, allergies to medication, and your current treatment.

Things To Have Before Taking A Cruise

- ☐ Copies of your prescriptions in case you may need an emergency refill. Bear in mind that many foreign countries may not refill your prescription.
- ☐ Two sets of medication. Carry one set with you and one set in your luggage.
- ☐ Enough medication to last longer than your entire cruise.
- ☐ An extra pair of prescription eyeglasses.
- ☐ Your physician's name and phone number in case of a medical emergency.
- ☐ If you think you will need it, bring sea sickness pills or a patch.
- ☐ A current major credit card.
- ☐ Extra batteries if you are hearing impaired.

Booking A Cruise

If you are considering taking a cruise, consider where you want to cruise and when you want to cruise. Read brochures about various destinations and amenities aboard the ship and at ports of call.

Contact a travel agent. Cruise lines only book through travel agents. You and your travel agent can select the cruise that meets your needs and wants. Inform your travel agent of the nature of your disability.

Your travel agent can call the cruise line, check space availability for the date you have selected, check for accessible cabin availability and determine the ship's requirements concerning your disability.

If you need an accessible cabin, try to book as early as possible because the number of cabins are limited. If an accessible cabin is not available for the cruise you have chosen, consider the best and largest outside cabin and try to book a cabin that is located midship.

It is recommended that you consider the newer and larger ships. These ships provide designated or accessible cabins near elevators, have wide hallways, low or no sills and accessible bathrooms. Remember, the larger the ship, the better the facilities, the more spacious the cabins and the more space in public and deck areas.

Transportation

Whether you are planning to travel by plane, train, bus or car to your port of embarkation, you should know how to travel with a disability. Knowing how to travel to your port of embarkation is just as important as cruising (See other transportation chapters).

If your cruise consists of an air/sea package, have your travel agent or the cruise line inform the air carrier providing the transportation of your disability and of your needs.

Ground Transportation

If you are unable to board the ground transportation provide by the cruise line from the airport to the ship, have your travel agent inform the cruise line that you will need an accessible van. You should also request the same service on your return.

Companion

Consider traveling with a companion to assist you in travel and aboard the ship. Many cruise lines require that you be accompanied by a companion because the crew is not permitted to escort you around the ship.

Insurance

Purchase cancellation insurance. The small premium you will pay will more than offset the price if you should have to cancel in case of an emergency. Your travel agent can provide details

Consider additional medical insurance. Medicare and many insurance companies that offer supplemental insurance do not extend coverage outside the United States.

Documentation

Have your travel agent check what documentation, such as a passport or visa, you will need as proof of citizenship.

Luggage

Don't try to bring everything from home. It is recommended that you travel with as little luggage as is necessary. You should travel with light, loose clothing and comfortable shoes for everyday wear. Information from the cruise line will indicate special theme nights and the form of attire required although not mandatory.

Embarking/Debarking

For the wheelchair passenger or the passenger with a mobility problem, have your travel agent check to see if you can board directly from the terminal or whether some other means must be provided. This also applies to debarking.

For the visually or hearing impaired passenger, a traveling companion can usually offer assistance in boarding.

Dining

If the ship offers two sittings for dinner, it is recommended that you select the second sitting for more leisurely dining.

If you are a wheelchair passenger, inform the maitre d' or dining room coordinator that you would like a table with plenty of room for your wheelchair, one that does not obstruct the waiters or other passengers.

You should, at the time of making your reservation, request whether you would like a table for two, four or more.

You can also receive special food service in your cabin, but why miss out on all the fun?

If you have need for a special diet or ethnic foods, your travel agent should inform the cruise line of your request.

Passengers With A Mobility Problem

If you are a passenger with a mobility problem but not in need of a wheelchair, try to book a cabin near an elevator. Walking down long, narrow hallways is no comfort.

The Wheelchair Passengers

Most cruise lines will require that you bring you own wheelchair. It is recommended that the wheelchair be lightweight, collapsible and non-electric. You should ask when booking, what type of wheelchair is accepted—regular or narrow. Elevator doors on many cruise ships are narrow and will not accommodate a regular wheelchair.

Check Cabin Accessibility

- Are there accessible cabins and where are the cabins located?
- Does the cabin have a riser or sill?
- Can ramps be provided to allow easy entry into the cabin and bathroom if there is a riser or sill?
- What is the width of the cabin and bathroom door?
- Is there enough room to maneuver a wheelchair in the cabin?

> Note: If you need a service animal, you must inform the dining facility or restaurant that you will be accompanied by a service animal. It is your responsibility to see that your service animal is under control at all times.

- Is the bathroom accessible with a roll-in shower or a hand held shower head?
- Does the bathroom door open inward?

For The Hearing Impaired Passenger

If you are hearing impaired, have a travel agent ask about assistive aids and devices such as:

- Assistive listening devices
- Closed captioned decoders
- Amplified telephones
- TDD/TTY service
- Visual alert systems

For The Diabetic Traveler

Your travel agent should inform the cruise line that you are diabetic and that you require refrigeration for your insulin. Also your travel agent should request a sugar-free diet. Carry several vials of insulin in case of breakage.

Traveling With A Service Animal

You must give advance notice if you are planning to travel with a service animal or guide dog. Some, but not all, cruise lines allow you to board with a service animal or guide dog. Have your travel agent check the cruise line for acceptability and their rules and regulations.

The care and feeding of your service animal or guide dog varies with the cruise line. On some ships, it is your responsibility to see to the care, feeding, handling and disposal of waste of your service animal or guide dog. On other ships, the cabin steward sees to the animal's feeding, walking and sanitation.

It is your responsibility to be informed about quarantine regulations for each country the ship calls on, and the inoculation requirements for re-entry into the United States with your service animal. Information on quarantine requirements and inoculation can be obtained from the national or state office of:

The United States Department of Agriculture
USDA, APHIS, VS
National Center for Imports & Exports
4700 River Road, Unit 39
Riverdale, Maryland 20737-1231
1-301-734-8590

Be sure to stipulate that you are inquiring about regulations for a service animal.

It is recommended that you inform the airlines and cruise lines that you are traveling with a service animal at the time of booking. Sometimes, airlines and cruise lines do not want a health certificate until ten days prior to departure.

Some cruise lines will require that the animal's food be sent directly to the ship prior to sailing. Other cruise lines will require 8 weeks notice so that the ship can supply the food, and the cost of the food will be applied to your on board account. You should have your travel agent check with the ship on food requirements for your service animal.

Traveling With Oxygen

You are required to get approval from the cruise line to travel with oxygen. You must give four to six weeks advance notice to the cruise line, prior to your sailing, that you will be traveling with oxygen. Approval can be obtained, depending on the cruise line, from the Special Service Department, the Customer Services Department, the Operations Department or the Passenger Courtesy Department.

You must supply your own oxygen and make your own arrangements to have your oxygen delivered directly to the ship. There are no refill facilities aboard the ship.

Some cruise lines will ask you to fill out a "Special Requirement Form" alerting the cruise line of your need to travel with oxygen.

You are required to have a written letter from your physician stating your ability to travel, a brief medical history and copies of your prescriptions.

Have your travel agent ask the cruise line if they have a list of oxygen suppliers at various ports of call. You will need a prescription from your physician indicating your need for oxygen and the liter- per-minute flow.

Most cruise ships will accept liquid oxygen systems on board the ship. Other cruise lines will require E-cylinders or L-30 containers. Your travel agent should check with the cruise line to determine which system is acceptable.

Before departure, inform your oxygen supplier of your travel plans including:

- Day of departure
- Day of return
- Sailing itinerary
- Method of transportation to your port of embarkation and returning home.

Your oxygen supplier can recommend the best system for travel and the amount of oxygen needed.

You should ask your oxygen supplier:

- To send a supply of oxygen directly to the ship prior to sailing.
- If oxygen refills can be arranged at ports of call, at the airport and port of embarkation.
- To give you the names of oxygen suppliers enroute, their locations, the refill charges and form of payment accepted

Have your physician give a prescription indicating your need for oxygen and the liter-per-minute flow.

Oxygen Check List

The following is a check list when planning to travel on a cruise with oxygen:

- ☐ Have I received permission from my physician to travel and cruise?
- ☐ Have I notified my travel agent that I will be traveling with oxygen?
- ☐ Have I obtained all necessary requirements from the cruiseship to travel with oxygen?
- ☐ Have I told my oxygen supplier of my travel plans including the means of transportation to the port of departure, date and duration of the cruise and means of travel back home?
- ☐ Do I have approval from the cruise line?
- ☐ Do I have enough oxygen for the length of the cruise and the names of oxygen suppliers and phone numbers at the port of departure and at ports of call?
- ☐ Do I have adequate medication, equipment and emergency information?
- ☐ Do I have enough oxygen to travel to and from home?

On-Board Guidelines

Consider traveling with a companion.

A ship is not required to provide you with personal needs such as feeding, dressing or toiletry.

The ship nurse or cabin steward cannot assist you in bathing, feeding, dressing, lifting or administrating routine medications.

You must be able to assist in your own evacuation of the ship in case of emergency.

You must be able to comprehend and respond to safety instructions from the crew.

Public And Deck Areas

On some ships, not all public and deck areas will be accessible if you are a wheelchair passenger. However, some areas could be made accessible if ramps are provided. Your travel agent can check CLIA'S "Cruise Guide for the Wheelchair Passenger" for the ships that list access to all areas.

Medical Services

Ships provide an infirmary with a doctor and nurse in attendance for minor medical service. If you require any medical attention, you will be charged for any service.

Features To Consider

Since the passage of the ADA of 1990, most new cruise ships are being built with features that make sailing accessible for the wheelchair passenger. Some older ships are being refitted with some of these same features.

Hearing Impaired Passengers

- Newer ships may be fitted with special colored signs.
- Some cruise ships offer headsets in their theaters.
- Some cruise ships offer closed-captioned television in cabins upon request.
- Ship announcements over the public address system may be difficult to understand.
- It might be difficult to use the ship's telephone service if it lacks a TDD system.
- Almost any inconvenience can be solved by traveling with an able-bodied companion.
- Bring extra batteries for your hearing aid.

- There may be designated or specially equipped cabins and public restrooms.
- Try to get cabins near elevators.
- Some ships have wider cabin and bathroom doors.
- Do cabins have grab bars for the bathtub, roll-in showers or handheld shower heads, accessible sinks?
- You can often get reserved seating areas to see shows and other entertainment.

It is recommended that your travel agent check for accessibility, but if the specific ship you have chosen to sail on is not wheelchair accessible be prepared to look for another.

Cruise Lines Terms And Conditions For A Passenger With A Disability

Each cruise line has its own terms and conditions regarding passengers with a disability. These terms and conditions are listed in the brochure printed by each cruise line. In general, the terms and conditions state:

Any medical or physical disability must be reported at the time the reservation is made.

Failure to provide such information could result in cancellation of the reservation.

A mentally impaired passenger will not be allowed to travel if he or she exhibits the type of anti-social (e.g. violent, seriously disruptive or illegal) behavior that would, under normal policy lead to removal from the ship.

The cruise line has the right to revoke or refuse passage to anyone, who in the judgment of the cruise line, requires treatment, care or attention beyond what the ship's facilities can provide, or if the passenger's mental or physical condition will not allow the passenger to participate in a cruise voyage.

The cruise line reserves the right to deny participation in certain activities.

The cruise line may require that the passenger with a disability be accompanied by an able-bodied companion who can provide assistance during the cruise and in case of an emergency

Passengers who use a wheelchair must provide their own small, collapsible wheelchair.

Cruise lines can require a passenger and companion sign a statement releasing the cruise line of any or all responsibility associated with the passenger's disability, relative to their ability to use shipboard facilities.

If a passenger has a mobility problem that does not require a wheelchair but is restricted in other ways, the cruise line must be notified in advance of sailing. The cruise line may request a letter from the passenger's physician that neither a wheelchair nor companion is needed, nor will the passenger require special attention on board.

Additional Considerations For Travel Outside The United States

If you are planning to travel outside the United States, check the following:

- ☐ Passport requirements

- ☐ Visa requirements
- ☐ Vaccination requirements
- ☐ Credit card requirements
- ☐ Rate of money exchange
- ☐ Weather and temperature
- ☐ State Department alerts that warn or forbid travel to certain countries.

Medical Insurance

Check medical insurance for coverage outside the USA. Medicare and many insurance companies do not extend coverage outside the USA. Purchasing medical insurance with your cancellation insurance could help defray the cost of medical treatment.

Epilogue

Yes, you have a disability. Almost everyone has *some* things they can't do. Some people have restrictions that are more severe than most. There are some things *you* can't do, or at least, you couldn't do without an impractical amount of effort or expense.

Having a disability doesn't have to mean that someone is disabled. You, too, can enjoy the pleasures of travel. Almost everyone can now, with the help of a more enlightened world, enjoy travel despite disabilities.

Don't neglect to take advantage of whatever pleasures are available to you. Work with your qualified travel agent to find the best way to enjoy the good things in life.

Things aren't always easy or perfect, but they are getting better. Let us all persevere in pursuing a world that is accessible to everyone—regardless of anyone's disabilities.

I hope, through this guidebook, to help you find and enjoy the best travel experience. If you have comments or suggestions for future editions, please address them to me, Fred Rosen, in care of Science & Humanities Press, PO Box 7151, Chesterfield, MO 63006-7151

Fred Rosen, Travel Consultant for Persons with a Disability

Resources

Books

Able to Travel: True Stories by and for People With Disabilities: A Rough Guide Special Published by Rough Guides, January, 1994. Paperback. ISBN: 1858281105. List: $19.95.

Fordor's Great American Vacations for Travelers With Disabilities (With Complete Accessibility Information on Hotels, Restaurants and Attractions) Published by Fordors Travel Publications, June, 1994. Paperback, 600 pages. ISBN: 067902591X. List: $18.00.

Mobility Training for People With Disabilities: Children and Adults With Physical, Mental, Visual, and Hearing Impairments Can Learn To Travel. Published by Charles C. Thomas Publishers Ltd, April, 1989. Hardcover. ISBN: 0398055726. List: $38.95.

The Physically Disabled Traveler's Guide. Published by Resource Directories, June, 1986. Paperback. ISBN: 0937521000. List: $9.95.

Travelability: A Guide for Physically Disabled Travelers in the United States. Published by Macmillan Publishing Company, December, 1978. Hardcover. ISBN: 0026011700. List: $13.95

Traveling . . . Like Everybody Else: A Practical Guide for Disabled Travelers. Published by Adama Books, September, 1987. Paperback. ISBN: 0915361779. List: $11.95.

Easy Access to National Parks: The Sierra Club Guide for People With Disabilities. Published by Sierra Arts Foundation, May, 1992. Paperback, 404 pages. ISBN: 0871566206. List: $16.00.

Directory of Travel Agencies for the Disabled. Published by Twin Peaks Pr., April, 1991. Paperback. ISBN: 0933261047. List: $19.95.
New Horizons for the Air Traveler With Disabilities. US. Department of Transportation. Office of Consumer Affairs, 400 Seventh Street, SW, Washington, DC. 20509 (202) 366-2200

Directory of Accessible Van Rentals. Published by Twin Peaks Press, 1992. PO. Box 129, Vancouver, WA 98666. Guidebook.

A World of Options for the 90's. Published by MIUSA, 1990. PO. Box 3551, Eugene, OR 97403. Travel Guide.

No Stairs to Climb in London. Author: Barbara Donchess. 1990. Travel Guide. Access guide for people who cannot climb stairs or walk long distances.

Periodicals

Access To The Skies, 801 Eighteenth Street, NW, Washington, DC 20006 Published by Paralyzed Veterans of America.

The Independence, PO. Box 1439, St. Charles, MO 63302-1439 Published monthly by JAG Enterprises. Subscription is $12.00 per year.

Handicapped Travel Newsletter, PO. Drawer 269, Athens, Texas 75751

Paraplegic News, 2111 East Highland Avenue, Suite 180, Phoenix, AZ 85016-4702 Published by Paralyzed Veterans of America, Inc.

I.V.U.N. News, from International Ventilator User's Network, Gazette International Network Institute, 5100 Oakland Ave, Suite 206, St Louis MO 63110-1406

One Step Ahead, A Resource for Active, Healthy, Independent Living, EKA Marketing, Inc, 9151 Hampton Overlook, Capitol Heights, MD 20743 800-386-5367

Organizations And Telephone Numbers

Government Agencies:

Department of Transportation, 400 Seventh Street SW, Room 10424, Washington, DC. 20590
(202) 366-9305 (202) 755-7687 (TDD)

Architectural and Transportation Barriers Compliance Board, 1111 18th Street NW, Suite 501, Washington, DC. 20036 800--USA-ABLE 800-USA-ABLE (TDD)

Rehabilitation Services Administration, US. Department of Education, Mary E. Switzer Building, Room 3028, 330 C Street, SW, Washington, DC. 20202-2531 (202) 732-1282

Administration on Developmental Disabilities, US. Department of Health and Human Services, Program Operations Division, 200 Independence Ave SW, Room 329D, Washington, DC 20201 (202) 245-2897 (202) 245-2890 (TDD)

Civil Rights Division, Office on the Americans with Disabilities Act, US. Department of Justice, PO. Box 66118, Washington, DC. 20035-6118 (202) 514-0301 (202) 514-0383 (TDD)

Disability--Specific

American Association of Respiratory Care 214-243-2272
11030 Ables Lane, Dallas, TX 75229

International Ventilators Users Network
5100 Oakland Avenue, Suite 206, St. Louis, MO 63110

National Information Center on Deafness
Gallaudet University, 800 Florida Avenue NE, Washington, DC. 20002

The Asthma and Allergy Foundation of America
1125 15th Street, Suite 502, Washington, DC. 20005

American Amputee Foundation 501-666-2523
PO. Box 250218, Hillcrest Station, Little Rock, AR 72225

American Civil Liberties Union AIDS Project 212-944-9800
132 West 43rd Street, New York, NY 10036

American Council of the Blind 202-467-5091

1115 15th Street NW, Suite 720, Washington, DC. 20005 ....
.... 800-424-8666

Epilepsy Foundation of America 301-459-3700
4351 Garden City Drive, Landover, MD 20785

American Printing House for the Blind 502-895-2405
1839 Frankfort Avenue, Louisville, KY 40206

National Federation of the Blind 301-659-9314
1800 Johnson Street, Baltimore, MD 21230

National Alliance for the Mentally Ill 703-524-7600
2101 Wilson Blvd., Suite 302, Arlington, VA 22201

National Association for the Physically Handicapped ....
4230 Emerick Street, Saginaw, MI 48602 517-799-3060

National Easter Seals Society 202-347-3066
1350 New York Avenue NW, Washington, DC. 20005 ....
.... 202-347-7385 (TDD)

Paralyzed Veterans of America 202-872-1300
801 18th Street NW, Washington, DC. 20006

Paraquad 314-567-1558
311 N Lindbergh Blvd, St Louis, MO 63141 ....
.... 314-567-5552 (TDD)

Project ACTION, National Easter Seal Society, 700 Thirteenth St NW, Suite 200, Washington, DC 20005 .... 800-659-NIAT

National Spinal Cord Injury Association 617-935-2722
600 West Cummings Park, Suite 2000, Woburn, MA 01801

National Rehabilitation Association 703-836-0850
633 South Washington Street, Alexandria, VA 22314

Business

US. Chamber of Commerce 202-463-5502
Labor and Human Resources Department
1615 H St. NW, Washington, DC. 20062

Legal

American Bar Association 202-311-2240
Commission on Mental and Physical Disability Law
1800 M Street NW, Washington, DC. 20036

National Disability Action Center 202-775-9231
1101 15th Street NW, Suite 1215, Washington, DC. 20005

American Arbitration Association 212-484-4060
140 West 51st Street, New York, NY 10020

World Wide Web

Alzheimer's Association .... http://www.alz.org/

American Cancer Society .... http://www.cancer.org/

American Council of the Blind .... http://www.acb.org/

American Diabetes Association .... http://www.diabetes.org/

American Foundation for the Blind .... http://www.afb.org/afb/

American Heart Association National ..... http://www.amhrt.org/

American Lung Association .... http://www.lungusa.org/

American Red Cross .... http://www.crossnet.org/

American Speech-Language-Hearing Association http://www2.asha.org/asha/

Arthritis Foundation .... http://www.arthritis.org

Bazelon Center for Mental Health Law .... http://www.bazelon.org/bazelon/

Center for Applied Special Technology ...... http://www.cast.org/

Children and Adults with Attention Deficit Disorder .... http://www.chadd.org/

Colorado Association of Community Centered Boards .... http://www.caccb.org/

Developmental Disabilities Resource Center .... http://www.caccb.org/ddrc/

Disabled American Veterans .... http://www.dav.org/

Disabled People's International .... http://www.dpi.org/

Families USA .... http://epn.org/families.html

Lupus Foundation of America ..... http://www.lupus.org/lupus/

Muscular Dystrophy Association .... http://www.mdausa.org/

National Ataxia Foundation .... http://www.ataxia.org/

National Center for the Dissemination of Disability Research .... http://www.ncddr.org/

National Federation of the Blind (NFB) .... http://www.nfb.org/

National Multiple Sclerosis Society .... http://www.nmss.org/

National Stroke Association .... http://www.stroke.org

One Step Ahead, A Resource for Active, Healthy, Independent Living .... http://www.disability.com/

Recording For The Blind & Dyslexic .... http://www.rfbd.org/

The New York Institute for Special Ed. ..... http://www.nyise.org/

United Cerebral Palsy .... http://www.ucp.org

United Way of America .... http://www.unitedway.org/

Veteran's Administration .... http://www.vvvc.org/

Appendix

Us Department Of Transportation

Information for the Air Traveler with a Disability

CONTENTS

Introduction

For years, access to the nation's air travel system for persons with disabilities was an area of substantial dissatisfaction, with both passengers and the airline industry recognizing the need for major improvement. In 1986 Congress passed the Air Carrier Access Act, requiring the Department of Transportation (DOT) to develop new regulations which ensure that persons with disabilities will be treated without discrimination in a way consistent with the safe carriage of all passengers. These regulations were published in March 1990.

The DOT regulations, referred to here as the Air Carrier Access rules, represent a major stride forward in improving air travel for persons with disabilities. The rules clearly explain the responsibilities of the traveler, the carriers, the airport operators, and contractors, who collectively make up the system which moves over one million passengers per day. (These rules do not apply to foreign airlines.)

The Air Carrier Access rules are designed to minimize the special problems that travelers with disabilities face as they negotiate their way through the nation's complex air travel system from origin to destination. This is achieved:

By recognizing that the physical barriers encountered by passengers with disabilities can frequently be overcome by employing simple changes in layout and technology.

By adopting the principle that many difficulties confronting passengers with hearing or vision impairments will be relieved if they are provided access to the same information that is available to all other passengers.

Through training of all air travel personnel who come in day-to-day contact with persons with disabilities, to understand their needs and how they can be accommodated quickly, safely, and with dignity.

This guide is designed to offer travelers with disabilities a brief but authoritative source of information about the Air Carrier Access rules: the accommodations, facilities, and services that are now required to be available. It also describes features required by other regulations designed to make air travel more accessible.

The guide is structured in much the same sequence as a passenger would plan for a trip: the circumstances he or she must consider prior to traveling, what will be encountered at the airport, and what to expect in the transitions from airport to airplane, on the plane, and then airplane to airport.

Planning Your Trip

The New Traveling Environment

THE AIR CARRIER ACCESS RULES SWEEP aside many restrictions that formerly discriminated against passengers with disabilities:

A carrier may not refuse transportation to a passenger solely on the basis of a disability.

Air carriers may not limit the number of individuals with disabilities on a particular flight.

All trip information that is made available to other passengers also must be made available to passengers with disabilities.

Carriers must provide passage to an individual who has a disability that may affect his or her appearance or involuntary behavior, even if this disability may offend, annoy, or be an inconvenience to crew-members or other passengers.

There Are A Few Exceptions:

The carrier may refuse transportation if the individual with a disability would endanger the health or safety of other passengers, or transporting the person would be a violation of FAA safety rules.

If the plane has fewer than 30 seats, the carrier may refuse transportation if there are no lifts, boarding chairs or other devices available which can be adapted to the limitations of such small aircraft by which to enplane the passenger. Airline personnel are not required to carry a mobility-impaired person onto the aircraft by hand.

There are special rules about persons with certain disabilities or communicable diseases. These rules are covered in the chapter entitled "At the Airport."

The carrier may refuse transportation if it is unable to seat the passenger without violating the FAA Exit Row Seating rules. See the chapter "On the Plane."

There Are New Procedures For Resolving Disputes:

All carriers are now required to have a Complaints Resolution Official (CRO) immediately available (even if by phone) to resolve disagreements which may arise between the carrier and passengers with disabilities.

Travelers who disagree with a carrier's actions toward them can pursue the issue with the carrier's CRO on the spot.

A carrier that refuses transportation to any person based on a disability must provide a written statement to that person within 10 calendar days, stating the basis for the refusal. The statement must include, where applicable, the basis for the carrier's opinion that transporting the person could be harmful to the safety of the flight.

If the passenger is still not satisfied, he or she may pursue DOT enforcement action.

Getting Advance Information About The Aircraft

Travelers with disabilities must be provided information upon request concerning facilities and services available to them. When feasible this information will pertain to the specific aircraft scheduled for a specific flight. Such information includes:

Any limitations which may be known to the carrier concerning the ability of the aircraft to accommodate an individual with a disability;

The location of seats (if any) with movable aisle armrests and any seats which the carrier does not make available to an individual with a disability (e.g., exit rows);

Any limitations on the availability of storage facilities in the cabin or in the cargo bay for mobility aids or other equipment commonly used by an individual with a disability.

Whether The Aircraft Has An Accessible Lavatory.

Normally, advance information about the aircraft will be requested by phone. Any carrier that provides telephone service for the purpose of making reservations or offering general information must provide comparable services for hearing-impaired individuals, utilizing telecommunications devices for the deaf (TDDs), or text telephones (TTs). The TTs shall be available during the same hours that the general public has access to regular phone service. The response time to answer calls on the TT line shall also be equivalent to the response time available to the general public. Charges for the call, if any, shall be the same as charges made to the general public.

When Advance Notice Can Be Required

Airlines may not require passengers with disabilities to provide advance notice of their intent to travel or of their disability except as provided below. Nonetheless, letting the airline know in advance how they can help you will generally result in a smoother trip.

Carriers may require up to 48 hours advance notice and one hour advance check-in from a person with a disability who wishes to receive any of the following services:

Transportation For An Electric Wheelchair On An Aircraft With Fewer Than 60 Seats;

Provision by the carrier of hazardous materials packaging for the battery of a wheelchair or other assistive device;

Accommodations For 10 Or More Passengers With Disabilities Who Travel As A Group;

Provision of an on-board wheelchair on an aircraft that does not have an accessible lavatory for persons who can use an inaccessible lavatory but need an on-board chair to do so.

Carriers are not required to provide the following services or equipment, but should they choose to provide them, they may require 48 hours advance notice and a one hour advance check-in:

- ☐ Medical oxygen for use on board the aircraft;
- ☐ Carriage of an incubator;
- ☐ Hook-up for a respirator to the aircraft's electrical supply;
- ☐ Accommodations for a passenger who must travel on a stretcher.

Carriers May Impose Reasonable, Nondiscriminatory Charges For These Optional Services.

Where a service is required by the rule, the airline must ensure that it is provided if appropriate notice has been given and the service requested is available on that particular flight. If a passenger does not meet advance notice or check-in requirements, carriers must make a reasonable effort to accommodate the requested service, providing this does not delay the flight.

If a passenger with a disability provides the required notice but is required to fly on another carrier (for example, if the flight is cancelled), the original carrier must, to the maximum extent feasible, provide assistance to the second carrier in furnishing the accommodation requested by the individual.

It must be recognized that even when a passenger has requested information in advance on the accessibility features of the scheduled aircraft, carriers sometimes have to substitute a different aircraft at the last minute for safety, mechanical or other reasons. It must also be recognized that the substitute aircraft may not be as fully accessible--a condition that may prevail for a number of years. Onboard wheelchairs must be available on many aircraft, but it will take a number of years before movable aisle armrests are available on all aircraft with over 30 seats. Similarly, while accessible lavatories must be built into all new wide-body aircraft, they will be put into existing aircraft only when such aircraft are undergoing a major interior refurbishment.

When Attendants Can Be Required

Carriers may require the following individuals to be accompanied by an attendant:

- ☐ A person traveling on a stretcher or in an incubator (for flights where such service is offered);

- ☐ A person who, because of a mental disability, is unable to comprehend or respond appropriately to safety instructions from carrier personnel;
- ☐ A person with a mobility impairment so severe that the individual is unable to assist in his or her own evacuation from the aircraft;
- ☐ A person who has both severe hearing and severe vision impairments which prevent him or her from receiving and acting on necessary instructions from carrier personnel when evacuating the aircraft during an emergency.

Recommendations

Tell your travel agent the nature of your disability and your travel needs. BE HONEST. Your travel agent wants to help you secure the accessibility you need but can only do so if your travel agent knows the nature of your disability.

Have your travel agent make the necessary reservations with your chosen mode of transportation or destination according to your form of disability. Make sure your travel agent asks the specific carrier or destination about their rules regarding travel with a wheelchair or oxygen.

Before departing, have your travel agent confirm that the selected carrier or destination has met your needs.

By knowing how to travel and being properly prepared, you can reduce the chance of something going wrong.

The carrier and the passenger may disagree about the applicability of one of these criteria. In such cases, the airline can require the passenger to travel with an attendant, contrary to the passenger's assurances that he or she can travel alone. However, the carrier cannot charge for the transportation of the attendant.

The airline can choose an attendant in a number of ways. It could designate an-off duty employee who happened to be traveling on the same flight to act as the attendant. The carrier or the passenger with a disability could seek a volunteer from among other passengers on the flight to act as the attendant. The carrier could provide a free ticket to an attendant of the passenger's choice for that flight segment. In the end, however, a carrier is not required to find or furnish an attendant.

The attendant would not be required to provide personal service to the passenger with a disability other than to provide assistance in the event of an emergency evacuation. This is in contrast to the case of the passenger that usually travels accompanied by a personal attendant, who would provide the passenger whatever service he or she requests.

If there is not a seat available on the flight for an attendant, and as a result a person with a disability holding a confirmed reservation is denied travel on the flight, the passenger with a disability is eligible for denied boarding compensation.

For purposes of determining whether a seat is available for an attendant, the attendant shall be deemed to have checked in at the same time as the person with the disability.

At the Airport

Airport Accessibility

UNTIL RECENTLY, ONLY THOSE AIRPORT facilities designed, constructed, or renovated by or for a recipient of federal funds had to comply with federal accessibility standards. Even at federally-assisted airports, not all facilities and activities were required to be accessible. Examples are privately-owned ground transportation and concessions selling goods or services to the public. (The accessibility features for over 500 airports are covered in a publication of the Airports Council International entitled Access Travel: Airports--A Guide to the Accessibility Of Terminals. It may be obtained by writing the Consumer Information Center, Pueblo, CO 81009.) As a result of the Air Carrier Access rules, and the Americans with Disabilities Act of 1990 (ADA) and implementing regulations, these privately-owned facilities must also be made accessible.

In general, airports under construction or being refurbished must comply with the ADA Accessibility Guidelines (ADAAG) and other regulations governing accessibility in accordance with a timetable established in the ADA. Thus, while there are still many changes to be made, the accessibility of most airports is improving. With few exceptions, the following services should be available in all air carrier terminals within the next few years:

- ☐ Accessible parking near the terminal;
- ☐ Signs indicating accessible parking and the easiest access from those spaces to the terminal;
- ☐ Accessible medical aid facilities and travelers aid stations;

- ☐ Accessible restrooms;
- ☐ Accessible drinking fountains;
- ☐ Accessible ticketing systems at primary fare collection areas;
- ☐ Amplified telephones and text telephones (TTs) for use by persons with hearing and speech impairments (there must be at least one TT in each terminal in a clearly marked accessible location);
- ☐ Accessible baggage check-in and retrieval areas;
- ☐ Jetways and mobile lounges that are accessible (at airports that have such facilities);
- ☐ Level entry boarding ramps, lifts or other means of assisting an individual with a disability on and off an aircraft;
- ☐ Information systems using visual words, letters or symbols with lighting and color coding, and systems for providing information orally;
- ☐ Signs indicating the location of specific facilities and services.

Moving Through The Airport

To make travel easier for an individual with a disability, major airports will be required to make the following services accessible under new rules being put into effect in the next several years:

Shuttle vehicles, owned or operated by airports, transporting people between parking lots and terminal buildings;

People Movers And Moving Walkways Within And Between Terminals And Gates.

All carrier facilities must currently include one accessible route from an airport entrance to ticket counters, boarding locations and baggage handling areas. Thes routes must minimize any extra distance that wheelchair users must travel compared to other passengers to reach these facilities. Outbound and inbound baggage facilities must provide efficient baggage handling for individuals with a disability, and these facilities must be designed and operated so as to be accessible. There must be appropriate signs to indicate the location of accessible services.

Carriers cannot restrict the movements of persons with disabilities in terminals or require them to remain in a holding area or other location while awaiting transportation and other assistance.

Curbside baggage check-in (available only for domestic flights) may be helpful to passengers with a disability.

Passenger Information

Carriers must ensure that individuals with disabilities, including those with vision and hearing impairments, have timely access to the same information provided to other passengers,including (but not limited to) information on:

- ☐ ticketing;
- ☐ scheduled departure times and gates;
- ☐ change of gate assignments;
- ☐ status of flight delays;
- ☐ schedule changes;
- ☐ flight check-in;
- ☐ checking and claiming of luggage.

This information must be made available upon request. A crew member is not required to interrupt his or her immediate safety duties to supply such information.

A copy of the Air Carrier Access rules must be made available by carriers for inspection upon request at each airport.

As previously noted, any carrier that provides telephone service for the purpose of making reservations or offering general information shall also provide TT service. This service for people with speech and hearing impairments must be available during the same hours that the general public has access to regular phone service, with equivalent response times and charges.

Security Screening

An individual with a disability must undergo the same security screening as any other member of the traveling public.

If an individual with a disability is able to pass through the security system without activating it, the person shall not be subject to special screening procedures. Security personnel are free to examine an assistive device that they believe is capable of concealing a weapon or other prohibited item. If an individual with a disability is not able to pass through the system without activating it, the person will be subject to further screening in the same manner as any other passenger activating the system.

Security screening personnel at some airports may employ a hand-held device that will allow them to complete the screening without having to physically search the individual. If this method is still unable to clear the individual and a physical search becomes necessary, then at the passenger's request, the search must be done in private.

If the passenger requests a private screening in a timely manner, the carrier must provide it in time for the passenger to board the aircraft. Such private screenings will not be required, however, to a greater extent or for any different reason than for other passengers. . However, they may take more time.

Medical Certificates

A medical certificate is a written statement from the passenger's physician saying that the passenger is capable of completing the flight safely without requiring extraordinary medical care.

A disability is not sufficient grounds for a carrier to request a medical certificate. Carriers shall not require passengers to present a medical certificate unless the person:

- ☐ Is on a stretcher or in an incubator (where such service is offered);
- ☐ Needs medical oxygen during flight (where such service is offered);
- ☐ Has a medical condition which causes the carrier to have reasonable doubt that the individual can complete the flight safely, without requiring extraordinary medical assistance during the flight; or
- ☐ Has a communicable disease or infection that has been determined by federal public health authorities to be generally transmittable during flight.

If the medical certificate is necessitated by a communicable disease (see next section), it must say that the disease or infection will not be communicable to other persons during the normal course of flight, or it shall state any conditions or precautions that would have to be observed to prevent transmission of the disease or infection to others.

Carriers cannot mandate separate treatment for an individual with a disability except for reasons of safety or to prevent the spread of a communicable disease or infection.

Communicable Diseases

As part of their responsibility to their passengers, air carriers try to prevent the spread of infection or a communicable disease on board an aircraft. If a person who seeks passage has an infection or disease that would be transmittable during the normal course of a flight, and that has been deemed so by a federal public health authority knowledgeable about the disease or infection, then the carrier may:

- ☐ Refuse to provide transportation to the person;
- ☐ Require the person to provide a medical certificate stating that the disease at its current stage would not be transmittable during the normal course of flight, or describing measures which would prevent transmission during flight;
- ☐ Impose on the person a condition or requirement not imposed on other passengers (.e.g., wearing a mask).

If the individual has a contagious disease but presents a medical certificate describing conditions or precautions that would prevent the transmission of the disease during the flight, the carrier shall provide transportation unless it is not feasible to act upon the conditions set forth in the certificate to prevent transmission of the disease.

Getting On And Off The Plane

The Safety Briefing

FAA REGULATIONS REQUIRE THAT carrier personnel provide a safety briefing to all passengers before takeoff. This briefing is for the passengers' own safety and is intended for that purpose only.

Carrier personnel may offer an individual briefing to a person whose disability precludes him or her from receiving the information presented in the general briefing. The individual briefing must be provided as inconspicuously and discretely as possible. Most carriers choose to offer this briefing before other passengers board the flight if the passenger with a disability chooses to pre-board the flight. A carrier can present the special briefing at any time before takeoff that does not interfere with other safety duties.

Carriers may not `quiz' the individual about the material presented in the briefing, except to the same degree they quiz all passengers about the general briefing. A carrier cannot take any adverse action against the passenger on the basis that, in the carrier's opinion, the passenger did not understand the safety briefing.

Safety briefings presented to passengers on video screens must have an open caption or an insert for a sign language interpreter, unless this would interfere with the video or would not be large enough to be seen. This requirement takes effect as old videos are replaced in the normal course of business.

Handling Of Mobility Aids And Assistive Devices

To the extent consistent with various FAA safety regulations, passengers may bring on board and use ventilators and respirators, powered by non-spillable batteries. Assistive devices brought into the cabin by an individual with a disability shall not count toward a limit on carry-on items.

Persons using canes and other assistive devices may stow these items on board the aircraft, consistent with safety regulations. Carriers shall permit passengers to stow wheelchairs or component parts of a mobility device under seats, or in overhead compartments.

Carriers must permit one folding wheelchair to be stowed in a cabin closet, or other approved priority storage area, if the aircraft has such areas and stowage can be accomplished in accordance with FAA safety regulations. If the passenger using it pre-boards, stowage of the wheelchair takes priority over the carry-on items brought on by other passengers enplaning at the same airport (including passengers in another cabin, such as First Class), but not over items of passengers who boarded at previous stops.

When stowed in the cargo compartment, wheelchairs and other assistive devices must be given priority over cargo and baggage, and must be among the first items unloaded. Mobility aids shall be returned to the owner as close as possible to the door of the aircraft (consistent with DOT hazardous materials regulations) or at the baggage claim area, in accordance with whatever request was made by the passenger before boarding.

If the priority storage accorded to mobility aids prevents another passenger's baggage from being carried, the carrier shall make its best efforts to ensure the other baggage arrives within four hours.

On certain aircraft, some assistive devices will have to be disassembled in order to be transported (e.g., electric wheelchairs, other devices too large to fit in the cabin or in the cargo hold in one piece). When assistive devices are disassembled, carriers are obligated to return them to passengers in the condition that the carrier received them (e.g., assembled).

Carriers must transport battery-powered wheelchairs, except where cargo compartment size or aircraft airworthiness considerations do not permit doing so. Electric wheelchairs must be treated in accordance with both DOT regulations for handling hazardous materials, and DOT Air Carrier Access regulations, which differentiate between spillable and non-spillable batteries:

Spillable Batteries. If the chair is powered by a spillable battery, the battery must be removed unless the wheelchair can be loaded, stored, secured, and unloaded always in an upright position. When it is possible to load, store, secure, and unload with the wheelchair always in an upright position and the battery is securely attached to the wheelchair, the carrier may not remove the battery from the chair.

Nonspillable Batteries

. It is never necessary under the DOT hazardous materials regulations to remove a nonspillable battery from a wheelchair before stowing it. There may be individual cases, however, in which a carrier is unable to determine whether a battery is spillable or nonspillable. DOT has issued new rules that require new non-spillable batteries to be marked as such effective September 1995.

The carrier may remove a particular unmarked battery from the mobility aid if there is reasonable doubt that it is nonspillable, and it cannot be loaded, stored, secured and unloaded always in an upright position. An across-the-board assumption that all batteries are spillable is not consistent with the Air Carrier Access rules.

A nonspillable battery may be removed where it appears to be damaged and leakage of battery fluid is possible.

Determining the Battery Type. Compliance with DOT rules on the marking of nonspillable batteries is sufficient to identify a battery as nonspillable for this purpose. In the absence of such markings, carrier personnel are responsible for determining, on a case-by-case basis, whether a battery is nonspillable, taking into account information provided by the user of the wheelchair.

The battery of a wheelchair may not be drained.

When DOT hazardous materials regulations require detaching the battery from the wheelchair, the carrier shall upon request provide packaging for the battery that will meet safety requirements.

Carriers may not charge for packaging wheelchair batteries.

Carriers may require passengers with electric wheelchairs to check in one hour before flight time.

If a passenger checks in less than one hour before flight time, the carrier shall make a reasonable effort to carry his or her wheelchair unless this would delay the flight.

Carriers must allow passengers to provide written instructions concerning the disassembly and assembly of their wheelchairs.

Carriers may not require a passenger with a disability to sign a waiver of liability for damage or loss of wheelchairs or other assistive devices. The carrier may make note of any pre-existing defect to the device.

On domestic trips, carriers' maximum liability for loss, damage or delay in returning assistive devices is twice the liability limit established for passengers' luggage under DOT regulations. As of the publication of this booklet, the current limit for liability on assistive devices is $2,500 per passenger (i.e., two times the $1,250 limit for luggage). (As with other passenger baggage, this limit can usually be increased by purchasing Excess Valuation coverage from the airline.) The passenger should also check his or her homeowners or renters insurance to determine whether it provides additional coverage.

This expanded liability does not extend to international trips, where the Warsaw Convention applies. For most international trips (including the domestic portions of an international trip) the current liability is approximately $9.07 per pound for checked baggage and $400 per passenger for unchecked baggage.

Boarding And Deplaning

Properly trained service personnel who are knowledgeable on how to assist individuals with a disability in boarding and exiting must be available if needed. Equipment used for assisting passengers must be kept in good working condition.

Boarding and exiting most medium and large-size jet aircraft is almost always by way of level boarding ramps or mobile lounges, which must be accessible. If ramps or mobile lounges are not used, a lifting device (other than a device used for freight) must be provided to assist persons with limited mobility safely on and off the aircraft.

For certain small aircraft, however, at present there are few suitable devices to assist persons with limited mobility in boarding and exiting. Lifting devices for smaller aircraft are now under development and will be put into place as soon as they become available.

Carriers do not have to hand-carry passengers on and off aircraft with fewer than 30 seats, if this is the only means of getting the person on and off the aircraft. Carrier employees may do so on a strictly voluntary basis.

In order to provide some personal assistance and extra time, the air carrier may offer a passenger with a disability, or any passenger that may be in need of assistance, the opportunity to pre-board the aircraft. The passenger has the option to accept or decline the offer.

On connecting flights, the delivering carrier is responsible for providing assistance to the individual with a disability in reaching his or her connecting flight.

Carriers cannot leave a passenger unattended for more than 30 minutes in a ground wheelchair, boarding chair, or other device in which the passenger is not independently mobile.

On The Plane

Aircraft Accessibility

PRIOR TO THE ENACTMENT OF THE AIR Carrier Access Act of 1986, accessibility requirements for aircraft were very limited. The rules implementing that law require that new aircraft delivered after April 1992 have the following accessibility features:

- ☐ For aircraft with 30 or more passenger seats: -- At least one half of the armrests on aisle seats shall be movable to facilitate transferring passengers from on-board wheelchairs to the aisle seat;
- ☐ -- Carriers shall establish procedures to ensure that individuals with disabilities can readily obtain seating in rows with movable aisle armrests;
- ☐ -- An aisle seat is not required to have a movable armrest if not feasible or if a person with a disability would be precluded from sitting there by FAA safety rules (e.g., an exit row).

For aircraft with 100 or more seats: -- Priority space in the cabin shall be provided for stowage of at least one passenger's folding wheelchair. (This rule also applies to aircraft of smaller size, if there is a closet large enough to accommodate a folding wheelchair.)

For aircraft with more than one aisle: -- At least one accessible lavatory (with door locks, call buttons, grab bars, and lever faucets) shall be available which will have sufficient room to allow a passenger using an on-board wheelchair to enter, maneuver, and use the facilities with the same degree of privacy as other passengers.

Aircraft with more than 60 seats must have an operable on-board wheelchair if

- ☐ There is an accessible lavatory, or
- ☐ A passenger provides advance notice that he or she can use an inaccessible lavatory but needs an on-board chair to reach it, even if the aircraft predated the rule and has not been refurbished (see below).
- ☐ An aircraft delivered before April 1992 does not have to be made accessible until its interior is refurbished. At that time the relevant accessibility features shall be added.

Airplanes in the commercial fleet have their seats replaced under different schedules depending on the carrier. At the time when all seats are being replaced on an aircraft with 30 or more passenger seats,half of the aisle seats must be equipped with movable aisle armrests. This shall be done on smaller aircraft to the extent it is not inconsistent with structural, weight, balance, operational or interior configuration limitations.

Similarly, all aircraft undergoing replacement of cabin interior elements or lavatories must meet the accessibility requirements for the affected features, including cabin storage space for a folding wheelchair, and an on-board wheelchair if there is an accessible lavatory (unless prohibited by structural, weight, balance, or configuration limitations).

Seat Assignments

An individual with a disability cannot be required to sit in a particular seat or be excluded from any seat, except as provided by FAA safety rules, such as the FAA Exit Row Seating rule. For safety reasons, that rule limits seating in exit rows to those persons with the most potential to be able to operate the emergency exit and help in an aircraft evacuation. The carrier cannot deny transport, but may deny specific seats to travelers who are less than age 15 or lack the capacity to act without an adult, or who lack sufficient mobility, strength, dexterity, vision, hearing, speech, reading or comprehension abilities to perform emergency evacuation functions. The carrier may also deny specific seats to persons with a condition or responsibilities, such as caring for small children, that might prevent the person from performing emergency evacuation functions, or cause harm to themselves in doing so.

A traveler with a disability may also be denied certain seats if:

- ☐ The passenger's involuntary behavior is such that it could compromise safety of the flight and the safety problem can be mitigated to an acceptable degree by assigning the passenger a specific seat rather than refusing service;
- ☐ The seat desired cannot accommodate guide dogs or service animals.

In each instance, carriers are obligated to offer alternative seat locations.

Service Animals

Carriers must permit dog guides or other service animals with appropriate identification to accompany an individual with a disability on a flight. Identification may include cards or other documentation, presence of a harness or markings on a harness, tags, or the credible verbal assurance of the passenger using the animal.

If carriers provide special information to passengers concerning the transportation of animals outside the continental United States, they must provide such information to all passengers with animals on such flights, not simply to passengers with disabilities who are traveling with service animals.

Carriers must permit a service animal to accompany a traveler with a disability to any seat in which the person sits, unless the animal obstructs an aisle or other area that must remain clear in order to facilitate an emergency evacuation, in which case the passenger will be assigned another seat.

In-Cabin Service

Air carrier personnel shall assist a passenger with a disability to:

- ☐ Move to and from seats as a part of the boarding and exiting process;
- ☐ Open packages and identify food (assistance with actual eating is not required);
- ☐ Use an on-board wheelchair when available to enable the passenger to move to and from the lavatory;
- ☐ Move to and from the lavatory, in the case of a semi-ambulatory person (as long as this does not require lifting or carrying by the airline employee);
- ☐ Load and retrieve carry-on items, including mobility aids and other assistive devices stowed on board the aircraft.

Carrier personnel are not required to provide assistance inside the lavatory or at the passenger's seat with elimination functions. The carrier personnel are also not required to perform medical services for an individual with a disability.

Charges For Accommodations Prohibited

Carriers cannot impose charges for providing facilities, equipment, or services to an individual with a disability that are required by DOT's Air Carrier Access regulations. They may charge for optional services, however, such as oxygen and accommodation of stretchers.

Personnel Training

Carriers must provide training on passengers with disabilities for all personnel who deal with the traveling public. This training shall be appropriate to the duties of each employee and will be designed to help the employee understand the special needs of these travelers, and how they can be accommodated quickly, safely, and with dignity. The training must familiarize employees with:

- ☐ The Department of Transportation's rules on the provision of air service to an individual with a disability;
- ☐ The carrier's procedures for providing transportation to persons with disabilities, including the proper and safe operation of any equipment used to accommodate such persons;
- ☐ How to respond appropriately to persons with different disabilities, including persons with mobility, sensory, mental, and emotional disabilities.

Compliance Procedures

EACH CARRIER MUST HAVE AT LEAST one Complaints Resolution Official (CRO) available at each airport during times of scheduled carrier operations. The CRO can be made available by telephone.

Any passenger having a complaint of alleged violations of the Air Carrier Access rules is entitled to communicate with a CRO, who has authority to resolve complaints on behalf of the carrier.

If a CRO receives a complaint before the action of carrier personnel has resulted in violation of the Air Carrier Access rules, the CRO must take or direct other carrier personnel to take action to ensure compliance with the rule. The CRO, however, does not have authority to countermand a safety-based decision made by the pilot-in-command of an aircraft.

If the CRO agrees with the passenger that a violation of the rule occurred, he must provide the passenger a written statement summarizing the facts and what steps if any, the carrier proposes to take in response to the violation.

If the CRO determines that no violation has occurred, he must provide the passenger a written statement summarizing the facts and reasons for the decision or conclusion.

The written statement must inform the interested party of his or her right to pursue DOT enforcement action if the passenger is still not satisfied with the response. If possible, the written statement by the CRO must be given to the passenger at the airport; otherwise, it shall be sent to the passenger within 10 days of the incident.

Carriers shall establish a procedure for resolving written complaints alleging violations of any Air Carrier Access rule provision. If a passenger chooses to file a written complaint, the complaint should note whether the passenger contacted the CRO at the time of the alleged violation, including the CRO's name and the date of contact, if available. It should include any written response received from the CRO. A carrier shall not be required to respond to a complaint postmarked more than 45 days after the date of an alleged violation.

A carrier must respond to a written complaint within 30 days after receiving it. The response must state the airline's position on the alleged violation, and may also state whether and why no violation occurred, or what the airline plans to do about the problem. The carrier must also inform the passenger of his or her right to pursue DOT enforcement action.

Any person believing that a carrier has violated any provision of the rule may report the incident to the following office:

Department of Transportation
Aviation Consumer Protection Division, C-75
400 Seventh Street, S.W.
Washington, D.C. 20590

In Conclusion

Our work is not yet done. At the time of publication of this booklet, there remained a number of accessibility issues unresolved. These include:

- ☐ Accessible terminal transportation systems;
- ☐ Boarding chair standards;
- ☐ Accessible lavatories on narrow body aircraft;
- ☐ Open captioning for in-flight movies and videos;
- ☐ TT service on aircraft.
- ☐ There are many others.

The Department of Transportation, along with groups representing people with disabilities and the air carrier industry, is dedicated to eliminating these barriers with all possible speed.

U.S. Department of Transportation

Check more information at

accessible-travel.com

Science & Humanities Press
(636) 394-4950

P.O. Box 7151
Chesterfield, MO 63006-7151
(636) 394-4950
http://www.sciencehumanitiespress.com

www.ingramcontent.com/pod-product-compliance
Lightning Source LLC
LaVergne TN
LVHW010102110826
845155LV00028B/453

* 9 7 8 1 8 8 8 7 2 5 0 5 6 *